WHEN THE WORLD WAS FAR AWAY

Ivy Fitzjohn

MINERVA PRESS
WASHINGTON LONDON MONTREUX

WHEN THE WORLD
WAS FAR AWAY

Copyright © Ivy Fitzjohn 1994

ISBN 1 85863 285 4

First Published 1994 by
MINERVA PRESS
10, Cromwell Place
London SW7 2JN.

Printed in Great Britain by
B.W.D. Printers Ltd., Northolt, Middlesex

WHEN THE WORLD WAS FAR AWAY

ABOUT THE AUTHOR

I grew up in Whittlesey, Cambridgeshire and attended school there before going on to the High School For Girls in the nearby town of March. After that, I worked for several years for the L.N.E.R (now part of British Rail) in Peterborough. In 1958, with my husband and two sons, I emigrated to Winnipeg, Canada, where I still live. After taking early retirement from the Manitoba Government's Social Services Dept. I spent much of my spare time writing. I have had numerous articles published, some of which have won prizes. When The World Was Far Away is my first published book. Initially written specifically for my family, it had appealed to other people as a nostalgic slice of social history. I have also written a novel, as yet unpublished.

TABLE OF CONTENTS

FOREWORD

During the fifty years that separate the childhood of myself and my generation from that of our grandchildren, greater changes have taken place than in any other half century period of history. Socially, medically, scientifically, technically and in many other respects, the world today is so far removed from the one in which we grew up that they appear to be separated by far more than a mere fifty years.

With our own roots firmly planted in a nostalgic era when we were able to shop for sweets or ice cream with only a halfpenny in our pockets, we have been propelled into an age in which money is casually discussed in units of billions, figures that during our childhood were considered so astronomical that it was difficult to contemplate ever actually budgeting such amounts, even at government level.

We find ourselves too, in an age of space exploration, computers and terrifying nuclear weapons that could be used to precipitate the entire world into annihilation.

Being an optimist, I prefer to think that civilisation will not self-destruct and that one day my grandchildren may become as curious about the life I and my generation lived as children as I have always been regarding the childhood of my own grandparents. My curiosity has had to remain unsatisfied to a large degree, but I often wonder about those little Victorians who became my forebears. I knew them well as adults, but wish I knew more of how they spent their time as children; the games they played, the books they read, what they learned at school, what kind of food they ate, what they wore, how they shopped and how they perceived the world around them.

We all have some knowledge of the Victorian era, but we know so little about the everyday lives of those particular, ordinary children who were destined to become our grandparents and great-grandparents.

Several years of diligent research by one of my sisters have produced a wealth of information on our family, covering a period of approximately two hundred years and fascinating it certainly is, an invaluable record to pass on to our children and grandchildren. We know the names of our ancestors on both sides of the family, where they lived, when and where they were born, when and whom they married, the occupations and trades they followed, when they died - and sometimes how - and many other intriguing facts and tid-bits of information.

After digging into the past few generations of my husband's family history and searching out old photographs and other material, I was able to assemble family history albums for our two sons, adding to the charts, photographs and pictures, a great deal of personally-remembered written material concerning grandparents, great-grandparents and other elderly and now-departed relatives.

Whilst involved in that project, it occurred to me that it would be of value to record at greater length an account of how we lived as children in a small, fenland town during the late 1920's and the 1930's. For the past thirty-five years (at the time I write this) I have lived some five thousand miles distant from that small town; my children have become Canadian citizens and my grandchildren are Canadian by birth.

This book is dedicated to them. It is also written for my seven brothers and sisters, the youngest of whom spent their childhood in a quite different world from mine. And it is also for my contemporaries, whom I trust will enjoy the nostalgia and the memories as much as I enjoyed recalling and writing about them.

* * * * *

SETTING THE SCENE

Whittlesey, like many fenland towns and villages, was once an island surrounded by meres and marshes that teemed with eels, fish and wild fowl, providing our forebears with food for themselves and a surplus to sell or barter for other necessities. There still remain many marshy areas, fringed by bulrushes and populated by ducks, geese and other water fowl.

When Dutch engineers began to drain the fens in the 17th century, fenmen sabotaged the building of the dikes for similar reasons that more than a century later, workmen in industrial cities sabotaged the new factories of the industrial revolution. People are almost always afraid when they see their lifestyle and their source of income threatened by technological progress. City dwellers of the late 18th and early 19th centuries saw their cottage industries doomed to extinction by the introduction of factory machinery, and fought a losing battle to hold on to the old ways.

Fenmen fought just as tenaciously to retain their independent way of life as harvesters of fish, fowl and the reeds and rushes that they used, or bartered to thatch dwellings, cover floors, weave into baskets and use for many other domestic purposes. Most of the older fenmen had no desire to become labourers on the farms that would flourish on the drained marshes, but eventually that would be the destiny of many of them.

Fenmen of past centuries adapted their lifestyle to suit their misty, marshy, watery land and throughout history travellers have commented on both the region and its inhabitants. In the year 1070 a Norman knight told William The Conqueror he had seen with his own eyes a thousand ducks taken from one mere and that he could scarcely believe there were so many fish and eels and fowl in all the world. He also described the abundance of deer, swine, goats and cattle, commenting that the animals needed no herding, their pastures being bounded by meres and lakes and dikes.

In 1560, during the reign of Elizabeth I, an unidentified traveller wrote: 'The inhabitants of the fenny country are a sort of people (much like the place) of brutish, uncivilised tempers, envious of all others whom they call upland men and usually walking aloft upon a sort of stilts. They all keep to the business of grazing, fishing and fowling. All this country in the winter time and sometimes for the greater part of the year is laid under water by the rivers, for want of sufficient passage.'

Many have written of the mists and fog that often covered the low-lying fens. Author Daniel Defoe was one, commenting in 1724: 'As these fens appear covered with water, so I observed too that at this latter part of the year they appear also covered with fogs and when the higher grounds of the adjacent country were gilded with the beams of the sun, the Isle Of Ely looked wrapped up in blankets, with nothing to be seen but now and then the lanthorn cupolas of Ely Minster.' He goes on to pity those who lived in the almost eternal mists and commented that many of the inhabitants suffered from the ague: "Which they make light of and there are great numbers of ancient people among them."

Before many of the counties of England were re-shaped, their names changed and their boundaries moved to suit the whims of modern planners, our county was known as The Isle Of Ely, an ancient name and one beloved by fen people; it is regrettable that such an historic county name will be allowed to fade into oblivion.

Even after the fens were drained, farmlands often flooded to a greater or lesser extent according to weather conditions and fenmen have had to wage a constant battle against flood waters on their low-lying, peaty, fertile farms and grazing land.

Whittlesey was mentioned in the Domesday Book of the 11th century, where it was referred to as Witesie; it then comprised a manor house, common grazing lands and farmland owned by the lord of the manor. The town's two churches, St. Mary's and St. Andrew's, frequently referred to when I was a child as the High Church and the Low Church (regarding liturgy, not height) both date from the 13th century. The soaring spire of St. Mary's is a landmark visible for miles around, while the solid, sturdy tower of St. Andrew's complements its sister church.

A few very old dwellings still survive in the town, the oldest reputed to date from the 17th century; it is now operated as a public house, complete with its own ghost that is said to manifest itself occasionally. Another, Portland House, home of the Earl of Portland during the commonwealth era of Oliver Cromwell, was a stone-built house close to both the old manor house and St. Mary's church. During the second world war, after standing vacant for several years, the house was converted into a hostel for members of the Land Army, a corps of mostly city-bred girls who worked on farms to replace local men who had joined the armed forces. When my mother was in her teens, she worked for a short period of time at Portland House as a nursemaid to two small girls whose father was an army officer stationed in India.

Portland House was demolished after the war and new houses built on the site. I recall hearing from my mother and other older people, stories of ghosts and monks and a secret underground passage leading to the church. There are several other interesting houses in the town, including a few built during the 18th century, their simple elegance still in keeping with modern buildings.

The ancient butter cross is a fine example of its type and standing as it does in the centre of the market place at the very heart of the town, lends an aura of age-old tranquillity that reflects the stoic, unruffled qualities of fenland people, who are not given to verbosity or impassioned action. They retain in their characters the independence of the island-dwellers of past centuries as well as the toughness and tenacity of Danish invaders to whom many owe the derivation of their names and often, their physical appearance. Few people of dark, sturdy, Celtic-like build are found among fen people. The Danes who ravaged and conquered brought with them their fair hair and complexions that predominate even today in many parts of East Anglia.

Like most towns we have our local heroes and heroines, but we also have a national hero, Lieutenant-General Sir Harry Smith, known as The Hero Of Aliwal after his notable success during the battle of Aliwal in the Sikh campaign in India during the 1840's. His name is now perpetuated in the name of a community college, a public house, a street and the house where he was born in 1788. His military career took him to many parts of the world including South America, The Netherlands, Spain, France, India and South Africa. During the Peninsular wars he married the daughter of a Spanish grandee and he served under the Duke of Wellington. His retirement was spent in Whittlesey until his death at the age of seventy-two. Both Sir Harry and Lady Smith are buried in Whittlesey cemetery. The town of

Ladysmith in South Africa, scene of a notable siege during the Boer war, was named after Sir Harry's wife and the nearby towns of Harrismith and Whittlesey were also named after the famous soldier.

Approaching the town, one is immediately aware of two of its major industries, agriculture and brick-making. The rich, fertile fen soil is spread before the traveller's eyes like a black carpet in winter, after the autumn ploughing and during the spring and summer months the green and gold of grain, sugar beet and other crops stretch for miles across the fens.

Rising like slim, brick towers above the flat landscape are the chimneys of brickyards that provide employment for a considerable number of men, though not as many as during my childhood days. Many of the old chimneys have now been demolished and yards closed, while others have been rebuilt below ground in the knotholes from which the clay is obtained for making bricks. The fortunes of the brickyards have wavered with the times. During the war, hundreds of thousands of bricks were stockpiled, due to a halt in building houses and other structures. At such times, men were laid off their jobs and the local economy waned, although in war time, men made munitions instead. When the economy booms, bricks are conveyed to every corner of the country and beyond, brickyards prosper and the men who make the bricks prosper along with them.

Clay is dug from enormous pits, known as knotholes, that dot the area; bricks are shaped, placed in kilns as blocks of wet clay and withdrawn as building bricks of varying colours and textures. Today, the process is mechanised in keeping with the times, but when my generation was young, much of the work was carried out manually and men sweated in the heat of the kilns or shivered in the damp, cold knotholes. Clay used to be loosened by pick-axe, then scraped from the sides of the knotholes by a shaler before being loaded into small, truck-like containers that swung along overhead cables to the yards where setters shaped the bricks in presses and wheel-barrowed them into the kilns where they were stacked for baking. Men known as burners started up the fires and watched over them day and night, controlling the temperature until the bricks were ready to be taken from the kilns. The men who carried out that task were called drawers; they spent their days wheel-barrowing bricks from the kilns and taking them to the stacking and loading zones. Theirs was perhaps the most enervating job in the yards and most drawers earned reasonably good money for those days. In summer they often began their day's work at the crack of dawn, finishing early in the afternoon in order to avoid working during the hottest part of the day. Men who worked in brickyards came home with their clothing covered in a reddish dust and in retrospect it would seem they must have inhaled a good deal of the choking dust, to the detriment of their lungs and bronchial systems.

Special rail sidings ran beside the kilns so that bricks could be loaded on to the flat rail cars ready for transportation to all parts of the country and sometimes to ports for transport overseas.

Bricks played an important part in many of our lives: our fathers and other relatives were employed in the industry and its ups and downs translated into highs and lows of family income. Our fathers sometimes brought home damaged bricks for use around the house and garden; one popular use was as a substitute for a hot water bottle on cold winter nights. Heated in the oven of the coal range, then wrapped in a thick piece of cloth, they remained hot for hours, keeping our beds warm in the unheated bedrooms. When we awoke in the morning they were still slightly warm and we could lie with our feet on the uncovered bricks before exposing our bodies to the chill, morning air.

Most of the brickyard workers, as did almost all manual workers of that era, cycled to work wearing peaked caps, heavy work boots, old clothing or overalls and with a bag, known locally as a dockey bag, containing their midday meal, slung over their shoulders. They froze in winter or were soaked by rain or groped their way through fog and mist or battled strong winds, but in summer the ride was almost a pleasure: *almost*, because there was always fatigue and the worry of making enough money to support their families.

Similarly dressed, the farm labourers of those days left their homes in the town or surrounding villages and set off for the fen farms where they toiled to earn a living. Many more people worked on the land then; few farms were mechanised and they required large numbers of workers to sow and reap and plough, to care for the animals and to maintain the farms. The horse was still supreme and the horsekeeper held one of the most important jobs on the farm. He had to be on his job earlier than most in order to feed his charges and prepare them for a day's field work. But all the men began their day early; they too, battled wind and rain and mist and cold in winter as they cycled along the often long, straight roads that unrolled like ribbons to farms and fields around the countryside.

Having reached the farm or the fields where they were to work, they propped their bicycles against a hedge or under a tree along with their dockey bag of food and drink, where it kept cool in summer and sheltered in winter. In cold weather they blew on their gloveless hands to warm them and flapped their arms around their chests to restore circulation after the cold ride in the thin, morning air. Then they were ready to begin their work. During haying and harvesting everyone was busy, wasting not a minute of sunshine or fair weather. In other seasons, work was determined by the skills of the men and the jobs to be done; ploughing, barrowing, hoeing, beet-topping, seeding, hedge-trimming, harvesting potatoes and stacking them into long, earth and straw-covered mounds along the edges of fields, from which they would later be taken as required for sale. Mangolds were harvested for cattle feed, acres of sugar beet harvested and transported to the local sugar refinery, other vegetables sown and hoed and picked or dug when ready as well as all the other thousand and one jobs that maintained fen farms and made them among the most productive in the world.

During harvest time the men worked late, often into the twilight hours, but in winter, when work was slow, they usually finished their daily chores by mid-afternoon and rode their bicycles home again, hoping that if they'd faced the wind in the morning it would not have change direction during the day to give them a hard ride home, stinging their faces or flinging icy rain at them as it swept across the bare, treeless fields. On very wet days they often couldn't work at all and precious wages were lost. Sometimes they sat in a barn or shed with sacks around their shoulders against the damp and cold, hoping the rain would stop, but if it didn't, they went home, losing a few hours pay. Some workers, those who lived in tied cottages that belonged to the farmer, paid low rents and often received produce such as milk or potatoes to supplement their wages, but others were not as fortunate and their families were among the poorest of those days.

Arriving home cold and hungry in winter, sweating and hot in summer, they sat down to a hot meal, known as a *cooked tea*, of good, filling suet pudding followed by a small portion of meat and plenty of home-grown vegetables. After a few hours rest and relaxation, perhaps on their own gardens in summer or dozing by the fire in winter, the labourers retired early to bed, in order to have a good sleep before the next hard day began.

Women made a major contribution to the agricultural industry, working in gangs on the farms to pick peas or potatoes, hoe crops, set out celery plants for market gardeners or to carry out any job that would release men for the heavier farm work. Wives of smallholders - and sometimes farmers' wives too - performed almost every task from milking cows and making butter to working in the fields, while at the same time keeping their farmhouses and cottages neat and tidy and providing filling meals for their men folk, who must remain fit and healthy to perform the hard work that never ended. Early every morning women could be seen setting out for work on the farms or market gardens wearing their old-fashioned, traditional print poke bonnets that protected their faces and necks from sun, wind and rain.

Not everyone worked in the brickyards or on the land, but those were the major sources of employment in the district. Some people travelled to the nearby city of Peterborough to work in factories, shops or offices, or they worked in local shops, offices or banks or they were employed by local tradesmen or perhaps owned their own businesses.

In those days the wheelwright and the blacksmith were still important figures. Walking past the blacksmith's forge as the big farm horses were shod, the acrid smell of burning assailed one's nostrils. Inside the forge, fanned into flames by bellows when necessary, the fire glowed, the blacksmith hammered on the anvil and the ringing sounds of iron on iron or steel were carried on the air as they had been for centuries. The wheelwright repaired farm wagons and wheels and also made new ones, painted in a bright orangy-red with the farmers' names in black letters on the sides of the wagons. They were displayed outside the wheelwright's workshop until the farmers were able to collect them and haul them off to farms for carting hay and grain and sugar beet and potatoes or other crops.

Baskets for potatoes and other vegetable crops were made for farmers and market gardeners by a local tradesman who also made shopping baskets and clothes baskets to hold heavy loads of laundry, other baskets for various purposes and even cradles for both babies and dolls.

Another important person was the saddler, who made and repaired equipment for farm horses, delivery horses and riding horses, though not many people in our area rode solely for pleasure. The saddler also sold the decorative brasses and other items used in preparing the magnificent Shires, Percherons and Suffolks that were shown in competition at agricultural fairs around the fens and indeed, all over the country, winning many prizes.

Like many other small towns and villages during that era, Whittlesey too, was diverse in occupations and industry and was to some extent, self-sufficient.

Being a fenland town we were subject to periodic flooding that covered large areas of surrounding farmland and grazing land. The town itself rarely flooded, though I do recall one year during my childhood when the flood waters reached part way into the town. It seemed exciting to me at the time, though it could scarcely have been so for those residents who had water lapping at their doorsteps.

With the floods that often occurred during the winter months, there sometimes came hard frosts that froze the flood waters and turned the countryside into a giant skating rink for a short period of time.

Fenmen have always been renowned for their speed-skating ability and as soon as the ice was thick enough to bear skaters, races were arranged and skaters dusted off their blades, eager to compete and demonstrate their skills. Not everyone was endowed with racing skills, but many skated anyway, provided they owned or were able to borrow skates, just for the fun of it.

Sometimes at weekends, entire families turned out to skate or slide or just to watch other people, creating a festive atmosphere. Some brought along old kitchen chairs to push along in front of them as they learned the tricky art of balancing on skates, while others wobbled along taking their bumps and falls as part of the fun and learning experience. Occasional winters produced extreme and persistent frosts when the rivers froze too and then the skaters sped along the rivers for miles. My husband, who lived in Thorney at that time, has told me he skated many times along the river and also used to skate on Whittlesey Wash with his parents and sisters. I never learned to skate, nor have I done so since; I'm quite content to watch others do so, surrounded as I am now each winter by people who grow up accepting ice and skating as naturally as they accept the changing of the seasons. Most Canadian children put on their first pair of skates at a very early age and few people grow up unable to skate at all.

One year, when I was about three years old, The Wash, as the grazing lands were known locally, flooded extensively, then froze hard so that hundreds of people for miles around turned out to enjoy the skating and sliding and the sport of all those acres of ice. My parents took me and my younger sister on a walk across the ice one afternoon. We had left our baby brother with our grandmother and I have a very clear remembrance of the four of us, my sister and myself holding hands with our parents holding our other hand, walking and sliding across the flooded, frozen fields. I'm not sure why they took us: perhaps they thought it would be an occasion we'd remember and if so, then I did indeed remember. Or perhaps, being young themselves, only in their early twenties, they wanted to participate in the fun of all that ice. We walked from the road, identifiable only by a line of pollarded willows, across the ice to where in summer, a gypsy encampment was always located. I still have a vivid memory of that day, our parents pulling us so that we slipped and fell and laughed our way along. I don't recall feeling cold, remembering only the vast expanse of ice and the enjoyment of what at the time seemed a special treat.

Today, Whittlesey, like towns everywhere, has new streets and new houses and has spread far beyond the boundaries we once knew. Old landmarks have disappeared, former country roads are now paved streets lined with houses and some localities have changed beyond recognition from the way we knew them as children. To recall them as they were then is to recall a totally different life style.

Many families in those days lived in small cottages, sometimes in enclosed courtyards known simply as *yards*, each with its individual name. A small alley led off the street, to all appearances the entrance to someone's back yard, but following the alley, or passage as it was usually known, one found oneself in an enclosed area with a few cottages surrounding or fronting on to the yard, the families living at very close quarters to each other. There were several such yards in the town and I always found them intriguing, they seemed so cosy and were usually neatly kept with small flower gardens. I liked the surprise quality of the yards, secret little streets hidden away from the main thoroughfares. There were also many rows of cottages along the streets themselves, most of them having only two rooms downstairs and two bedrooms upstairs, yet families with several children lived in many of those small dwellings. The majority of the cottages have now been demolished to make way for new development, the families having moved to new, subsidised council houses or perhaps, in a few cases, having bought their own homes.

The cottages of our day were attractive from the outside but many lacked the most basic conveniences and space was very limited. Outdoor toilets were often shared by more than one family and a water pump in the communal back yard provided the water supply for several families. Those pumps sometimes froze in winter and many a frosty morning was enlivened by curses as householders carried out kettles of boiling water to free up the pump. Many families ensured an early morning water supply by filling kettles the previous night.

Despite the inconveniences, most of the cottages were well-maintained; indeed many of them were spic and span with polished windows, whitened steps and shiny brass doorknobs. The rooms inside were for the most part, as neat as the proverbial new pin, with a bright fire burning in a shiny black grate, polished furniture and despite a lack of cupboards and closets, an appearance of order and comfort. There were always a few families however, where the mother was unable to cope with poverty, a large family or perhaps an uncooperative husband in such a small space. Or perhaps she herself was the product of a deprived home, and overwhelmed by circumstances, was incapable of overcoming them and attaining standards set by her neighbours. She was sometimes condemned as slovenly. In retrospect, perhaps such sad situations were cries for help, but in those days there was no generous government department to hand out financial assistance, nor was there sufficient moral support.

A very elderly relative of mine, a great-great-aunt, lived in a perfect example of the small cottage, one of a row of four. A blank wall faced on to the street, but on walking down a side passage, one entered a tiny yard, where the windows of the four cottages faced small gardens backed by a row of wash houses, coal sheds and earth closets. Those cottages were smaller than most, having only one tiny room downstairs and an equally small bedroom upstairs. My old aunt, who owned the cottages, did in fact live in two of them, the lower rooms having a connecting door, but what always fascinated me was that a doorway had never been made between the bedrooms and they remained isolated from each other, each with its own staircase.

There was a Victorian aura about everything; pictures, furniture (including a prickly, horse-hair sofa), a huge family bible on a side table, knickknacks everywhere and a trellis of purple clematis around the doorway. Aunt herself dressed in voluminous black garments that would have been fashionable during Queen Victoria's life time and like the old Queen, she wore a bead-trimmed black bonnet when she went out. Beneath the bonnet she wore a wig to cover her almost bald head. She lived well into her nineties and left a house stuffed with books, jewellery and other relics to be sorted, distributed or thrown away. Some of the items thrown away might well have been valuable as antiques today! My youngest sisters and their friends played dress-up games for years after Aunt's death with her bonnets and capes and old-fashioned accessories.

Some of the older cottages in the town had thatched roofs and I recall a spectacular fire that burned a row of them to the ground, forcing the occupants from their homes with the loss of many of their possessions. Thatching has always been a local craft, carried on mainly by one family who were renowned all over the country for the skill of their workmen, who travelled far and wide to repair and install thatched roofs. There are still a few excellent examples of the craft to be seen locally.

There used to be a few very old dwellings built with mud-like walls, sometimes called wattle and daub. They were formed from a mixture of mud and straw or reeds, dating from centuries past, an example of using whatever material was at hand. Sometimes the walls were white-washed, giving them a stucco-like appearance. There were also some walls in the town built in the same manner, and a sample of this has been preserved for future generations. The walls were sometimes topped with thatch, like a narrow roof, to protect them from crumbling due to rain and the erosion of time.

The age-old custom of building from materials at hand has always been a factor in man's adaptation to his environment: fenmen of the past used to build dwellings of turves, dug from the land on which their primitive shelters stood. The same type of building material was used by pioneers in North America, where it is called sod.

Immigrants who homesteaded on the prairies in both Canada and the United States stacked the sods to make solid - if sometimes cold - dwellings and filled the gaps between the sods with mud. In forested regions, where lumber was available for the cutting, pioneers built log cabins, many of which have been preserved as historic reminders of the past.

Not everyone lived in cottages, but because it is a form of housing diminishing year by year, it seems relevant to dwell on it to some extent. In our childhood, as is true today, dwellings were of all sorts and sizes, from subsidised council houses built and rented by local authorities, to genteel detached and semi-detached villas, converted railway coaches, accommodations adjoining businesses, houses of character both large and small and elegant houses owned by affluent families. Many houses used to be given names, it was considered rather smart and a way of emulating those who lived in the Big Houses that have always, traditionally, been known only by name. As the town grew postal authorities insisted on all houses using a street number, but many also retained their names and it is still interesting to walk along streets and read them; they were often derived from a combination of family names or were named for a vacation spot enjoyed by the family, or perhaps even a battle or historic name.

I was always fascinated by houses of all kinds and whenever possible, enjoyed glimpses into them, whether they belonged to friends, relatives or strangers. Passing by houses when lights were lit but curtains still undrawn, I peeped into rooms to see what the interiors were like. I often felt envious of what I saw and vowed to myself that one day I would have a house with carpets and elegant furniture and lovely pictures and vases of flowers and simple, tasteful ornaments. I suppose I have acquired some of those items!

Not only buildings and history, but people too, contribute to the character of a town and Whittlesey had several residents who fell into that category. Not always important personages, they were nevertheless people who in some manner are remembered for their personalities, flamboyancy, their contribution to local society or their work on behalf of others. Some of those persons who added flavour to the community during my childhood are recalled in specific roles or situations that either affected or impressed me and though I am able to recall their appearances, voices and mode of dress, some of their names have been forgotten over the years. Some were well known to only a few residents, others were known by almost everyone.

One such person was Mary - not her real name - an ageless retardate who spent much of her time wandering up and down the main street talking to shopkeepers and anyone else she could engage in conversation. She may perhaps have been somewhat of a nuisance on occasions, but few really objected to her and like many retardates, she was happy most of the time. Her loud, hearty laughter could be heard as she was playfully teased and chased away from premises or as she called out to friends and passers-by. Occasionally she took it into her head to perform an impromptu dance in the middle of the street and was not adverse to lifting up her skirts, swirling them around her waist in her exuberance. She was also often to be found in the foyer of the cinema, where she loved to gaze at pictures of film stars or talk to the proprietor and to patrons as they entered for the evening's showing.

Another character was a man I, and many others, knew only as *Flowery George*. I recall him as middle-aged, wearing a suit that had seen better days, a rusty-black bowler hat and almost always, whatever the weather or time of year, an over-sized boutonniere in his lapel. Who he was, whether he worked or had a family or where he lived, I never knew. He was the butt of many jokes, but I have a feeling he enjoyed his notoriety. He was usually in evidence on busy days such as market day, parading along the street, tipping his hat to ladies as he passed.

Someone who may not have been a character in the accepted sense of the word but who was a person *of* character was a middle-aged, unmarried lady who acted as a foster-mother to boys from an orphanage or boys' home. She usually had two or three boys at any given time and I remember them as well-cared for and happy, yet also disciplined. They were usually dressed in grey flannel shorts, matching grey shorts and pullovers and often wore grey felt panama hats of the type sometimes worn at that time by young boys. I can see them now, neatly-dressed, arms swinging as they marched along beside their foster-mother, a small, slim lady with a no-nonsense, but kindly manner and a brisk step that could easily match that of the boys as she led them along for all the world like a mother hen with a line of chicks.

Reggie Perkins was a vendor of fruit, sold from a pushcart. Piled with oranges, apples, bananas and sometimes more exotic fruit and sweets, he wheeled his mobile fruit market around the town, selling his wares. I particularly recall him standing outside the cinema in Market Street on Friday and Saturday evenings, doing brisk business with patrons on their way to an evening out. Occasionally he called out his wares to attract customers, who often seemed to be young men who gathered around his cart, chatting to him as they made purchases, teasing him in a good-natured manner. He was a small man of indeterminate age, with a cheerful countenance and a walk reminiscent of Charlie Chaplin.

We had a town crier who in those days occasionally exercised his lungs to make announcements. Hearing his bell and the ancient cry of: Oyez, oyez, we rushed to the market place to discover what important item of news was about to be imparted, but more often than not, it turned out to be a request from a local farmer for women to work on his farm or perhaps an announcement regarding an up-coming local event or attraction. Real news, the prerogative of town criers of past centuries, was by then obtained from newspapers or by radio, but the old cry could still attract a crowd to listen to even the most commonplace announcement.

We were all very class-conscious in those days: both the old-established families representing affluence and the upper crust of local society were often regarded with awe. They were perceived almost as superior beings, mixing for the most part with their own kind and speaking in accents that set them apart. Their children attended boarding schools and were seen only during school holidays; the men were solicitors, doctors, or followed other professions and the families often lived in large houses set in lovely grounds. Most of those people however, worked very hard to make life a little better for families experiencing hard times. They gave generously of their time to local organisations, charities, churches and other groups, sat on school boards and acted as justices of the peace, became involved in supporting local events and opened their gardens in summer for band concerts and garden fetes.

There were only a few such families but they worked willingly and untiringly to improve the lot of their less fortunate neighbours. Usually well educated, they were social workers in the true and traditional sense, often visiting the poor and sick, donating food and clothing and demonstrating a genuine compassion and concern for victims of those depressed years. Many local people were perhaps unaware of the extent of their involvement in such work, which was often carried out unsung and behind the scenes, but I recall several such kindnesses to my own family and they have not been forgotten.

Several other townspeople whom I recall as having made an impression on my childhood self, will be summoned from the depths of my memory in later chapters of this narrative, in the context in which they belong and are fondly remembered.

There were many others, ordinary people whose names I either never knew or have now forgotten, who remain frozen in the 1930's, forever cast in the role they then occupied, appearing as they did then, speaking the words they spoke then, their individualism providing colour and character to the town and adding to its social history. The real essence of a community is always in its people.

* * * * *

THE TONE OF THE TIMES

Our childhood was spent between the wars, that last period of peace and innocence before The Holocaust and The Bomb, before television brought violence and crime and sex into our homes, before the world came and sat on our doorsteps and refused ever to go away again. When my generation were children the world seemed very far away, brought to us second-hand through books, newspapers and magazines, glimpses of newsreels at the cinema and through the then new medium of radio.

Many of our fathers, grandfathers and uncles had experienced the horrors of the trenches during the 1914-18 war, but we had been born a few years after it ended and for us that terrible war was filed away in our minds with the Boer and Crimean wars, with Waterloo and The Armada. We sang *Pack Up Your Troubles* and *Tipperary* and *Mademoiselle From Armentieres*, but they ranked in our minds with music hall songs and evoked no personal memories as they did for the war veterans and their families. When *they* sang those songs they thought of Verdun, Mons, Ypres and The Somme and they remembered the mud and the barbed wire and poppies growing in Flanders' Fields.

When as children we read the names of the dead on the war memorial it seemed merely an alphabetical list, the names having no meaning because we had never seen those men in the flesh. We wore poppies on Armistice Day and knew the reason why, but we didn't experience the sadness and heartbreak of that poignant day. For our elders, the memories were still vivid and part of the recent past. Such experiences were yet to come for us, sooner than we then realised, but mercifully still unthought of. Most people at that time were struggling to survive the tough decade that preceded the second world war.

The experiences of our childhood took place within the narrow confines of our small, fenland town, with occasional forays outside its boundaries to shop, spend a day at the seaside, visit relatives and for a few, to spend holidays. It was all we knew or wanted, to us it was the world and the events that occurred therein were as shattering, as exciting, as happy or as sad as any that took place in the larger world of which we then knew so little.

Our world was tougher than today's in that we owned so few of the material possessions now considered essential for survival, but we never perceived ourselves as poor, poverty being a relative state. Even affluent families had no electrical appliances with which to wash and dry laundry, preserve and freeze food, toast bread and take care of all those tasks that today's marvels of technology perform for us so effortlessly and efficiently. True, affluent families employed women to do their laundry, maids to houseclean, nursemaids to care for their children and sometimes cooks to prepare their meals, but that was an accepted fact of life and provided employment for working class members of society.

Travel, for many people, was limited to seaside holidays or visits to relatives or friends. For the privileged few who were able to travel abroad, the mode of travel was by sea and over land; the ocean liners and trains of the civilised world offered the ultimate in comfort and luxury during that era. Aircraft were slow and cumbersome, developed very little since the first world war. If one flew over, we rushed outside to watch, commenting on whether it was a biplane or a monoplane. Often, the small aircraft flew just above the treetops and one could see the pilot at his controls. Sometimes we even knew whose plane it was and who was flying it. We followed with bated breath the adventures of pioneer aviators such as Amy Johnson and Jim Mollison as they flew hazardous missions over oceans and around the world in their fragile flying machines. We'd never heard of jet engines and travel by passenger aircraft flying regular routes was almost as remote a prospect as the possibility of being projected into space.

The pace of life was leisurely: children played safely in the streets; cows were driven through the streets to pasture each morning after the early milking and driven home again late in the afternoon, often by a boy on a bicycle, before and after his day at school. There was sometimes a brief episode of excitement - even temporary panic - when a cow became bored with the same old daily routine and decided to walk through a temptingly-open gate to trample carefully-tended flowers or vegetables. After a chase by the cowhand, accompanied by colourful language and mooing protests by the animal, the errant bovine was rounded up and sedately resumed her walk to the milking sheds or pasture.

Travelling to Peterborough, seven miles distant, on market day, it was not uncommon to encounter a flock of sheep or herd of cattle being driven to market for sale. They almost blocked the road, causing buses and other vehicles to nose their way through the living mass of beef or mutton on the hoof at walking pace, the sheep especially living up to their reputation as stupid animals, insisting on remaining almost beneath the wheels of passing traffic. Traffic was fortunately far less dense in those days.

Education, for the majority, meant leaving school at fourteen and finding a job, either locally or in Peterborough. The choices were limited, as was the opportunity for advancement. Most young people had to settle for being employed as a shop assistant or errand boy, farm labourer or press boy in the brickyards, an apprentice in a factory or a family business, as a maid, nursemaid or other domestic with an affluent or status-seeking family. Office jobs were for the most part filled by the fortunate few who had attended high schools or grammar schools or by those who had taken a commercial course after leaving the local secondary school.

Few pupils advanced to university or training college; that was a privilege available only to an extremely small minority. Few families could afford to support a son or daughter for such a long period of time, even though there were many who were academically suited to higher education and would have liked to pursue a scholastic career. Even leaving school at sixteen after attending high school or grammar school was considered a luxury; tactless, unkind remarks were sometimes made to and about some of those young people. I know! I was on occasion the recipient of remarks such as: A big girl (or boy, as the case may be) like that still at school! Imagine the guilt one felt on being told, indirectly but pointedly, that one was an unfair burden on one's parents. The pressure was on everyone from working class families to get a job as soon as possible and bring in extra money to help out with the family budget. For many, there was no question of their keeping all, or even most of their wages for clothes, records, cosmetics, jewellery or other such personal acquisitions taken for granted by today's teenagers. The lion's share of the new earner's wage was handed over to Mother to be incorporated into general household expenses, with just enough retained to pay for bus fares and small personal items. Clothing was often purchased from family funds.

Wages were ludicrously low, even allowing for the galloping

inflation that has taken place since then. Most young people earn more in one hour today than their counterparts in the 1930's earned in a week. Girls working in service, the term then used for domestic work, started at about five shillings per week, though that amount varied, depending on the employer and whether or not the domestic servant lived in or was employed on a daily basis. Errand boys and girls beginning as shop assistants were usually paid seven shillings and sixpence a week and apprentices in trades usually received nothing; they often paid for the privilege of learning a skill or trade. Young people starting in offices were considered well-paid at between ten and fifteen shillings weekly. Employers did not often promote girls to better-paid positions; their jobs were for the most part considered stop-gap positions until they married. Babies usually arrived early in marriages and few women worked outside the home, at least in the type of jobs they'd previously held. Many of them were employed as seasonal workers by farmers or market gardeners, or they worked as domestic help, earning part time incomes to subsidise their husbands' wages and enabling them to buy a few extras for their children, additional items for the home or even to pay off a doctor's bill. No one complained about all this, it was the way life was ordained and was accepted thus. Not until after the war started in 1939 and the manufacture of munitions and other war time products got under way did wages increase and the old order begin to crumble.

Wages may have been low during the decade preceding the war, but prices were also correspondingly low. A family man might earn three or four pounds per week, but a house could be rented for a few shillings. Farm labourers earned much less, except perhaps at harvest time and other peak periods of the agricultural year, but some lived in tied cottages paying little or no rent and received potatoes and milk to eke out their budget. Still, they were among the very poor and even better-paid labourers had little or no money left over each week for luxuries. A hundredweight sack of coal cost about two shillings and since in many homes most of the cooking was done on a coal range, little other fuel was required. From ten to sixteen eggs could be bought for one shilling, varying according to the time of year; pork sausage was one shilling per pound and staples such as sugar and flour cost only a few pennies per pound. It was still hard to stretch the money from week to week. There were few luxuries; meat was served in very small portions, cakes bought from the baker were a special treat, as was a meal of fish and chips or tins of fruit with cream out of a tin for tea. If things got really tight, one could always make a stew of sixpenny worth of "pieces" from the butcher, eked out with plenty of vegetables and suet dumplings.

Every penny counted. Families were often large, men were sometimes out of work for lengthy periods of time and received only dole money with which to support their families. Due to a poor diet and in some cases, inadequate clothing, or even if that were not a factor, due to the lack of both medical knowledge and effective drugs, there was frequent illness, especially among children. Doctors' bills mounted - no free health service then - and often had to be paid off in instalments over long periods of time.

Running a home required sheer stamina; there were few labour-saving appliances and a mother's work went on from early morning to evening. The constant worry of providing nutritious food and warm clothing was a bogey stalking many parents. Some local clothiers and outfitters operated clubs, whereby a weekly payment could be made, usually a shilling or two, so that there was always credit available to purchase essential items or to cope with emergencies. This worked both ways: by retaining the weekly payments, retailers were assured the money would be spent at their shops. Clothing was passed down in families, as it still is today, exchanged with relatives or friends, altered to fit someone else or made at home on the old Singer treadle or hand sewing machine.

Food for the most part was plain but adequate: we ate little meat, but suet or milk puddings filled up the corners at dinner time and there was always plenty of bread and home-made jam for tea. Bread was good in those days, freshly baked each day and with a texture, flavour and aroma that has long since disappeared with the introduction of mass-produced, sliced, wrapped bread of the variety sold in modern supermarkets. There are still small bakeries that bake good, old-fashioned bread but sadly, they are becoming fewer.

Men who worked in the brickyards or on farms carried a "dockey" of thick slices of bread topped with a chunk of cold roast meat, fat bacon or cheese; it was wrapped in a clean cloth and often accompanied by a bottle of cold tea to wash the meal down. They cycled to and from work on dark winter mornings and afternoons with carbide lamps to light their way; in time, battery-operated lamps and then dynamos made their appearance, improving both vision and safety.

    We dressed differently from today's children: jeans, expensive running shoes and easily-washed and dried clothing of man-made fibres were unknown in the 1930's. Boys wore flannel shorts held up by striped, S-buckled belts, knee-high wool socks with turned down striped tops and for school, they usually wore boots. Only a few boys wore shoes, always referred to as *low shoes* by both men and boys, as opposed to boots that reached above the ankles. Boys rarely graduated to long trousers until they were about fourteen years old and the ritual of wearing that item of men's' wear for the first time was an adolescent rite. With their shorts they wore either a shirt and blazer or a woollen jersey with a collar and matching, woollen tie with horizontal stripes. Those jersey and tie sets were displayed in every shop that sold boys' clothing.

    Girls never wore slacks, even for casual wear; they weren't even available. For school we wore a skirt or gym tunic with a blouse, or perhaps a dress made of serge, soft wool or stockinette. In winter we often wore wool stockings and if it was very cold, younger girls often wore gaiters, now an obsolete item of dress. They were made either of fleecy-lined stockinette or for those who could afford it, leather; they reached from ankle to just above the knee, with elastic under the shoe to keep them in place. They were a bother to get on and off, they fastened with little buttons all the way down the side and it was an exasperating performance to fasten and unfasten them, especially when one's hands were cold. Zippers were in their infancy, so we wore almost nothing that zipped. Snap fasteners, buttons and hooks and eyes were the order of the day. Beneath our winter clothing we wore an assortment of bodices, vests and petticoats to keep out the damp, penetrating cold and we wore sensible shoes and felt hats or berets.

    In summer we wore cotton dresses that our mothers spent hours ironing with flat irons. Boys wore thin, short-sleeved shirts and khaki cotton drill shorts. Our summer shoes were canvas, unless our parents considered them bad for our feet; white for girls, and brown or black for boys.

    Some items of clothing were status symbols. I always longed for an accordion-pleated skirt, a furry, "teddy bear" coat, kid-palmed gloves with astrakhan backs, ankle-strap, black patent leather shoes, anything knitted from fluffy, angora wool, a winter dress trimmed with swansdown and almost anything that was pretty and dainty and impractical.

Our vocabulary was limited compared with today's knowledgeable, media-oriented children, and many words now in daily use would have been completely alien to us. If we had been asked for instance, to go "shopping for a pair of nylon tights", "a polyester shirt and plastic bowl", to call at the "supermarket" for "frozen fish sticks" and a packet of "frozen peas", then check at the "electronic appliance shop" to inquire if the repairs to our "television" set had been completed, we would have gaped in astonishment. We'd never heard of nylon, polyester or plastic; frozen food was unknown and what on earth was a television set? For that matter, what was a supermarket? Television and its allied invention, radar, were in fact a glimmer on the horizon at that time, but news of such a magical method of entertainment and communication had not penetrated to our small corner of the world.

Space was an invention of H.G. Wells, and astronauts were the imaginary men who inhabited that fictitious place. The moon was where the man in the moon lived, or an object the cow jumped over; a missile was an object thrown at something or someone by someone else; a computer was a person who added up figures; nuclear was an unknown word and we were taught that the atom was unsplittable.

Few people in the 1930's talked, or even thought much about the environment. Thousands of house chimneys emitted smoke from coal fires into the atmosphere and local brickyard chimneys belched their gaseous smoke over the town. In winter, smoke mingled with fog, and the mists indigenous to the damp, low-lying fens formed a smoggy compound that we unconcernedly inhaled, never suspecting it may be responsible for at least some of the wheezing, coughing and chest complaints suffered by many in that region, especially the elderly. Even so, we were more fortunate than many city-dwellers, hemmed in as they were by smoke-belching factories. Now, with an enforceable government act that bans smoke-producing fuels to a large extent, we have cleaner air to breathe and fewer old people die of congested and poisoned lungs.

Teenagers hadn't been invented when we were young, nor vandalism as we now know it. Young people were busy earning a living by the time they were fourteen, or if they were lucky, sixteen and saw themselves as young adults. Of course there were law-breakers and they were dealt with by the law; those who annoyed or trespassed or stole were punished by the victim or by their parents or even by a policeman and no one accused the disciplinarians of child abuse. If you had no more sense than to get into trouble, you paid the price. Policemen were the law and were respected; no one fought them in demonstrations or street battles. Teachers used a cane or their hand to keep order in the classroom; a few of them went too far and hit out to vent their own anger and they were feared, but for the most part discipline was reasonably good and few pupils caused trouble that teachers were unable to deal with.

In those days, before the media intervened in our speech patterns and we were perhaps not as well-informed as we are today, the fen dialect was far more prevalent, especially among older inhabitants, but to a lesser extent among young people too. We weren't supposed to pronounce some of our words the way we did; parents and teachers alike pounced on us to *speak properly*. Nonetheless, we mimicked or inherited many dialect words and expressions. If we were very scared of something, we were *frit to dead;* when we were very cold, we were *frez*. It was still common to hear words such as *like* and *bike* pronounced *loike* and *boike*. Many older people referred to *home* and *stone* as *hum* and *stun*; country folk often said *larn* and *arn* and *charch* instead of *learn* and *earn* and *church*; *chairs* were sometimes *cheers* and the words *can't* and *shan't* were sometimes pronounced *cain't* and *shain't*. Some verbs were given distinctive past tenses, as in it *snew* for it *snowed* or he *hew* the onions instead of be *hoed* them. An interesting use of the word *time* was prevalent among some elderly folk. They often said: *Time* I was gone, meaning *while* I was gone or: *Time* I get back, meaning: *When* I get back. The word time in these contexts are abbreviations of *During the time* and *By the time*.

Hollywood, brought to us via the courtesy of our local cinema, began to invade our speech and the English language was never quite the same again. One heard such expressions, now long outmoded even in their native Hollywood, as *Swell* and *Okay big boy* and the perennial *Stick 'em up!*

Speech today is far less class-oriented than it used to be and it is becoming more difficult, for the most part, to categorise a person by the manner in which he or she speaks. Dialects are gradually becoming modified or even eroded by better education, travel, the influence of radio and television and a desire on the part of many people to shake off an accent that may prove an impediment to their career.

Our grandchildren will probably view us in retrospect as naive and unworldly children and our life style as primitive in comparison to theirs. Certainly we were less confident than they are and we were more in awe of authority. They travel the continent and the world with as little concern as we travelled to the seaside or to a big city for an outing or holiday. They accept their computerised, technological age as casually as we accepted our age of manual labour and horse power and they accept the world as we accepted our small town.

In the following chapters I have tried to recapture some of the elements of the world of our childhood, to recall some of the every-day events, customs, people, places and memories. It is a personal remembrance, viewed from my standing as the eldest child of a large family. I have interspersed the narrative with personal and family anecdotes that I trust will add emphasis or humour, or in some manner accent a situation or event.

The socio-economic standing of my family was working class, with an ancestry on one side of independent, self-employed business men and women; on the other side, generations of country dwellers, the salt of the earth. We were always urged to pull ourselves up by our bootstraps, to compete, to open every door and to make something of ourselves.

Many readers, even members of my own family, will remember different events from those years, or they may recall the same events in a different context.

Whatever your memories are of your own childhood during those years, I invite you to accompany me on a nostalgic journey, back to the days when I was a child and the world was very far away.

* * * * *

THE MARKET PLACE

For centuries our market place has been the focal point around which events, both important and commonplace, have unfolded. Like the spokes of a wheel, several streets converge on to it and by moving a few paces this way or that, one can look along any one of the streets.

The ancient butter cross with its stone pillars stands four square in the centre of the market place and has its own long history. Generations before our time farmers and their wives travelled from outlying fen farms to sell their dairy and farm produce, sheltered from the elements under the steep roof of the butter cross. Farmers met there to sell their oats, wheat and barley and to compare crops and discuss current affairs; and the butter cross has presided over markets and fairs, celebrations and parades and has provided shelter from sudden showers, from summer heat and winter rain or snow.

The market place is referred to by some older residents as "The Market Hill" or simply "The Hill". They've always congregated there to discuss everything from crops to the weather, from the high cost of living to inadequate wages, from wars to politicians and to make comments on the passing scene, their conversation economical in the fen tradition.

"Noice day," was the usual greeting by locals to a stranger or to each other. Strangers were welcome to listen to the regulars' conversation and proffer an occasional comment, but the men would have been embarrassed by too much talk. Animated, excitable verbal expression was acceptable from some people: Irish labourers, for instance, who appeared every summer during our childhood to work on farms at harvest time were known to have the gift of the gab; conversing at length with conviction and authority was right and proper too, coming from educated people who were involved in local affairs, the church, or who were considered scholars. But working class fenmen were not talkers: their conversation comprised for the most part, brief remarks and comments, each of their companions fully understanding the intent and feelings of the speaker. Their ancestry of life on remote farms and islands was still inherent in their phlegmatic, often withdrawn nature. Energy had always been conserved to survive, to fight invaders or to conquer the elements and natural disasters. Speech was superfluous. The Fen Tiger could be a merciless foe or a fiercely protective friend and ally, but he was uneasy with words.

"I'm going up The Hill," was a farewell remark that must have been spoken from time immemorial by men to their wives on Saturday evenings as they left to meet their cronies. During my childhood, older men stood under the butter cross dressed in collarless, striped shirts, flat cloth caps and sometimes wearing a red and white cotton handkerchief, that they called a *neckercher*, knotted around their throats. Family men in tidy but sometimes shabby clothes tried to forget for an hour or two, as they chatted with their mates, the heavy family responsibilities that lay on their often young shoulders. Rattling loose change in their pockets, all that was left after handing over most of their weekly wage to their wives for rent, food and clothing, they envied the young bloods in their flashy suits and long, fringed, white silk scarves as they crossed the market place to The George or The Angel. Spilling out from the pubs later in the evening, merry on a few pints of mild or bitter, the youths crossed to the fish shop, pushing and jostling each other good-naturedly, to buy newspaper-wrapped cod and chips, well salted and vinegared; the aroma drifted over to the men who could no longer afford such luxuries.

Some men, instead of standing under the butter cross, preferred to congregate outside The Angel, on the corner of Eastgate and High Causeway, to survey the market place from a different viewpoint. They stood in a line, along the High Causeway side of the pub by choice, obtaining a good view down Market Street. Late arrivals had to settle for the less prestigious Eastgate side. Seeing them standing there in line, heels on the path, toes pointing down into the gutter, usually wearing dark clothing, I was always reminded of birds perched along telephone wires, gathering for their annual flight south for the winter. Hands tucked in trouser pockets, the men exchanged news, guffawed over a joke or discussed the ever-present problem of unemployment. Occasionally, one of the men daringly called out a cheeky or even a mildly ribald remark to a female passer-by, causing the more conservative among the group to grin and shuffle uneasily until the subject of the remark had disappeared from sight.

Now and then one or two of the men broke ranks and entered The

Angel for their Saturday night pint or half pint and a game of darts or dominoes, a beery smell emanating from the barroom each time the door opened. On cold, wet or foggy nights the rest of the men soon dispersed. Some, supporting families on the dole, had no overcoats and their thin clothing was no protection against the penetrating, damp cold of a late, fen evening. A few may have been wearing the poor man's insulation of sheets of thick, brown paper inside their shirts. Like cardboard insoles in boots and shoes, it was not uncommon in those depression years.

The market place on weekdays was part of the town's shopping scene and housewives on foot, on bicycles or pushing babies in prams crossed the square from street to street or entered the post office that faced on to the market square. Old people went in to collect their weekly pension, some to buy postal money orders for their husbands' weekly flutter on the football pools and others to mail letters or parcels. Almost everyone stopped to chat with friends and acquaintances whom they met as they went about their business. Children on their way to and from school enlivened the air with their chattering, laughing and squabbling as they crossed the market place morning, lunch time and afternoon.

It was on Fridays that the market place really came to life. Friday was, and still is, market day. There has been an established market in the town since 1770, though it's almost certain that people sold their produce there for centuries before that. Today's market is but a vestige of those that were held between the two world wars. Then people travelled from fens and farms and surrounding villages to the market that was a busy, crowded, exciting event.

I remember it best on summer afternoons and winter evenings. During the summer holidays, after midday dinner on Fridays, my mother washed and dressed us to a shining cleanliness, we girls in starched dresses and whitened, canvas shoes with white socks, the boys in clean shorts and shirts. We walked to the market to look around the stalls and make a purchase here and there, if the price was right. Often, we encountered aunts and cousins who had come into town from their fen smallholdings to do their weekly shopping; they always complimented my mother on our immaculate appearance, but we shrank shyly from their efforts to engage us in conversation. They seemed so much larger than life, those friendly, older aunts, but we listened with fascination to their talk, their speech having a more pronounced fen dialect than most people who lived in the town.

For many mothers market day was an opportunity to relax for an hour or two, to escape from housework and child-caring; they stopped frequently to chat as they met friends and relatives on their circuit of the market stalls, enjoying the social aspect of the afternoon outing as much as the more necessary task of comparing prices and stretching the housekeeping money.

I very much enjoyed listening to those adult conversations, even though I was sometimes puzzled by their content and at times, the tone of voice the speakers used, adding an air of mystery to the exchange of information. On one specific occasion, when as usual I'd been listening to my mother and a friend discussing a topic that probably wasn't - to me - particularly interesting, I suddenly heard a comment that sent shivers down my spine and to this day I can pinpoint exactly where we were standing at the time. As they chatted away, oblivious of my rapt attention, a young woman walked past and my mother's friend remarked, "That's Miss So-And-So. Poor thing, she just lost her mother."

From the pleasantry of idle listening I was jolted into a horrified awareness. *Lost her mother?* How could anyone lose their mother? I turned to look at the subject of the comment, but saw only an ordinary woman, not the kind of person who would lose a mother. Suppose *our* mother became lost! Mentally, I panicked, imagining myself, my brothers and sisters left as semi-orphans, with no one to look after us. Life without a mother was too terrible to contemplate.

I remember worrying about that overheard conversation for a long time afterwards, sometimes even thinking about it on my way home from school and running the rest of the way to make sure my mother was still there. I don't recollect ever discussing the incident with anyone, probably not really wanting to know how such a situation could occur. Eventually my fear faded, but the remembrance has remained with me to this day, a reminder of how easily a chance remark can be misinterpreted by a child.

I liked the market best of all on winter evenings. My father often used to go after tea and sometimes took me along with him. We would set out, warmly wrapped against the damp and cold of the evening and after walking through the darkness of Blunt's Lane, emerged into the brightness of High Causeway, busy with shoppers and lit by shafts of light from shop doorways along the street. Everything was so different after dark: discarded pieces of orange peel stained puddles with rainbow colours as oil met water, but I didn't know there was oil in orange peel and wanted to know why it made colours. My father didn't know either. On frosty evenings a thin, transparent crust of ice formed on puddles in the gutter and the temptation to step down and crack the film of ice with my shoe was irresistible; it made a fine network of cracks over the surface, like an icy cobweb.

As soon as we reached Ailsby's chemist shop we could see ahead of us the naphtha flares that lit the market stalls; and the milling crowds, breath issuing from their mouths into the frosty air like dragons breathing fire. Once into the melée of people and stalls and shouting vendors and hissing flares it seemed festive, exciting and magical. We stopped first to watch the escape artist writhing to free himself from a straight jacket and chains that had been bound around him by his partner. The audience held its breath as he struggled valiantly, playing to the crowd; then with a flourish he threw up his arms and cast off his bonds. Everyone clapped and many stayed to see what his next feat would be.

We moved on to watch the Pot Man, joining the crowd standing in a circle around him. Plates and dishes, cups and bowls, jug and wash basin sets and chamber pots were arranged in a large circle on the ground. The Pot Man himself stood in the centre of the circle like a circus performer, while the audience stood outside the circle of wares. Deftly spreading plates and saucers along his arm like a magician with a pack of cards, he expounded on their beauty, wearability and value as he proceeded to lure potential buyers. He started off with a high price, gradually reducing it to the amount he knew he could get and customers would be willing to pay. It was all part of the fun and the sales pitch. He made jokes about chamber pots, drawing raucous but embarrassed laughter from his audience and entertained them with his deftness and patter. Before long, he and his assistant were wrapping tea sets and dinner plates and bowls and passing them into the crowd, money being passed hand over hand back to him.

We toured the rest of the stalls, stopping for a few minutes here and there to listen to the sales patter of vendors of clothing, jewellery, household items and other goods of all kinds, each stall attracting a crowd of spectators, many of whom were out for an evening's entertainment rather than an evening's spending. Many of the stallholders were as funny and entertaining as professional comedians.

Some of the largest crowds gathered around the fruit vendors and we eventually made our way there too, hoping to take home a bargain bag of fruit. There were usually two or three vendors, selling from their lorries, vying with each other for business as they bargained with the waiting crowd. They shouted friendly insults to each other and tried to outdo each other in the amount of fruit they were prepared to sell - give away, they insisted - for one shilling. Paper carrier bags were gradually filled with oranges, an apple or two, perhaps a couple of bananas and sometimes even a small bunch of grapes to top it off. Sometimes it was just oranges, small and sweet and juicy. The crowd held back, waiting for the rock bottom price that would eventually be negotiated and then the shillings were produced, bags of fruit passed overhead to those at the back of the crowd and finally everyone received their prize to take home, convinced they'd bought the best bargain ever. We began to think of home too, holding tight to our bag of oranges that would soon be shared with the rest of the family around a glowing fire. But first, we visited the pork butcher's stall to buy a few pennyworth of cracklings; small, crispy morsels remaining after fat had been rendered for lard. They were delicious when eaten with new, crusty bread. Indigestible perhaps, but cheap and tasty, a treat to be enjoyed the following day.

Two or three times each year a fair came to town, the biggest one being the Statute Fair in the autumn, known locally as *The Statice*. At such times the market place was transformed into a noisy, exciting fairground. A few days before the fair was scheduled to start, caravans belonging to the fair owners and work crews began to arrive, to settle in for their brief stay. In those days most of the old-established fair families still used horse-drawn caravans, gleaming with bright paintwork and shiny brass, neatly and meticulously maintained both inside and out. Many of them parked along one side of a street that faced my grandfather's grocery shop and I found it endlessly fascinating to watch their comings and goings and listen to their conversations when they came to the shop to buy groceries. My grandparents came to know most of them by name over a period of several years and they and the fair people greeted each other like old friends. In addition to the little homes on wheels, the large trucks and trailers rumbled in, loaded with the bare bones of stalls and rides and all the machinery and parts required to set up a fair.

On our way to and from school each day we watched the stalls and side-shows, the roundabouts and swing boats gradually take shape as the expert crews and mechanics deftly and swiftly assembled the numerous parts as easily as though they were pieces of a giant Meccano set. The colourful fair people in their bright, casual clothing seemed like foreigners to us or a little like gypsies. The big showman's engine that provided power for the lights and the rides soon pulsated away and music was tried out, sounding somewhat out of place in the middle of the day.

By Friday the fair was ready to go, though workers were usually still completing some of the attractions and putting last minute touches to everything. During the afternoon, parents took young children for penny rides on the "little roundabouts", manually operated by a man standing in the centre of the circle of painted ponies, bicycles, cars and aeroplanes. A few of the side-shows were in operation, but it wasn't until the evening, after dark, that the fair really came to life.

On Friday evening, when it was also market day, market stalls were set up along Market Street, giving up their regular sites to the fair. Pennies had been saved to spend on the rides, sometimes augmented by relatives or older brothers and sisters, for those who had them. From streets away one could hear the throbbing of the power engine, the blaring music, the screams of the riders on the fast roundabout and the general crowd noises as well as the cries of side-show operators and stall vendors. Before trying anything or spending money it was essential to walk around and inspect everything: the undulating, breath-taking speed of the big horses with their brass poles, the swing boats, rocked and pumped high in the air by daredevil youths and girls, the bumper cars, the vibrating, joggling cakewalk. Among the side-shows not to be missed were the shooting gallery with balls suspended above jets of water, coconut shies at which local muscle men tried their hand at knocking the coconuts off their stands, the prize for doing so being the coconut itself, a treat to be shared at home with the rest of the family. We always hoped our Dad would bring one home and he often did so. Darts, throwing rings around objects and rolling pennies were all played in tests of skill or luck to win one of the cheap, junky prizes of dolls, stuffed toys or garish ornaments.

There were shows too: attractive, scantily-clad girls gyrated on a small platform to lure customers into a tent where the show took place, a barker expounding on the wonders to be seen for the price of admission. Often it was a fat lady, a man with an extra hand, an animal with two heads, a Tom Thumb-like midget or other such abnormal creatures of the human race or animal world. Those people made a living exhibiting themselves; today, such displays of deformity are rare, yet at that time few people gave it a second thought, or if the thoughts were there, they did not voice them.

A fortune-teller sat in a small tent, peering into a crystal ball on a table before her. Velvet curtains formed a door and were opened just enough to show a tantalising glimpse of the exotic, gypsy-like figure inside. Prospective clients hovered outside, trying to summon the courage to enter and hear prophesies of handsome strangers, good luck and wonderful futures the dark lady would predict for them.

One of the most popular of the regular vendors, welcomed at every fair, was The Rock King, an outsize man with an outsize personality, an outsize moustache and always wearing a wide-brimmed western-style hat. He presided over piles of nougat, coloured rock candy, Turkish delight and many other delicious sweets. His brandy snap, delicate, hollow cylinders of a crisp, fragile, toffee-like confection that melted in one's mouth, were the best I ever tasted. A few pennies bought only a minimal amount of his delicious concoctions, but they were pennies well spent.

For two nights the fair cast its spell over the market place, luring stolid citizens to abandon their usual reserve and join in the revelry of rides and marksmanship and fun. Long after we were in bed we could hear the throbbing of the music reaching us on the late night air and we lay wishing we were old enough to stay at the fair until midnight, to be part of the magic, the bright lights, swishing roundabouts, ugly prizes, laughter and excitement. We were unable to sleep as we relived our own few hours spent there earlier in the evening.

By the following morning most of the fair had already disappeared. Trucks had been loaded overnight with dismantled machinery, animals from the rides, tents and prizes, skeletons of stalls and all the hundred and one items that had comprised the temporary, tinselly attraction. The horses had been brought from their pasture, hitched to caravans and once again the fair was on its nomadic way to another town, leaving us with only memories until it returned the following year.

On Sunday mornings the market place exuded a serene atmosphere after the busy Friday and Saturday shopping days.   Church bells pealed out melodiously across the town, summoning parishioners of both churches to morning service. A few men leaned on bicycles near the butter cross, idly watching people, dressed in their Sunday-best outfits, on their way to church.   Others pedalled their bicycles leisurely along, perhaps on their way to visit parents or friends, while other men wandered across to pubs for a drink before returning home for the traditional Sunday dinner.

Early in the evening, the Salvation Army corps marched along Market Street playing a rousing tune, often *Onward Christian Soldiers*, halting at the market place to hold their evening service. Mocked by some, those admirable Christians held strong convictions of their beliefs, and played and sang cheerful hymns regardless of what others thought of them.   There were local men though, those who had been through the hell of The Great War, who knew that the Salvation Army not only sang hymns and wore old-fashioned uniforms, but knew how to act in an old-fashioned Christian manner. Pressing as close to the front line as they were allowed, they had provided welcoming cups of tea, sandwiches and buns to men numbed and exhausted and in shock from battles that seemed to have no end.

There were certain Sundays during the year when the market place became the focal point of special events. On Whit-Sunday, there used to be a parade of all the Sunday schools in the town, of all denominations; similar parades took place in many other towns and cities too.   Each Sunday school had an identifying banner carried at the head of the group by a teacher or member of the school.   It was traditional for children to wear white, in keeping with the Pentecostal holiday being celebrated.   The parade was led through the town, headed by a band, then returned to the market place, where a brief service was held before the parade disbanded. I recall taking part in the Whit-Sunday parade a few times before the custom died out a few years before the war.

Hospital Sunday was another local event held until some time during the 1930's.   Prior to the National Health Service system, hospitals were supported to some extent by public donations and Hospital Sunday was an annual event held to raise funds. On the Saturday evening a parade through the town gave a send-off to the fund-raising, it also being an opportunity to canvas the shopping and cinema-going crowds, many of them from country areas. Participants in the parade dressed as clowns or in other comical costumes, stopping to speak to children along the route, while at the same time rattling their collection boxes at the parents. We used to call the clowns *The Funny Men*. On the Sunday, there was a band concert and a service on the market place, with donations again being solicited. I recall seeing photographs taken on those Sundays, some of them before my time, when the crowds were very large indeed, filling the market place.

The most impressive recollection I have of the market place is of the service held there every year on the Sunday afternoon closest to Armistice Day. In the early 1930's the memories of The Great War were still very vividly entrenched in the minds of everyone who had lived through those years; most of all in the minds and hearts of the survivors who had fought in the battles of the war that was to have ended all wars.

On November 11th, the remembrances were more individual, more private; services were held in schools, everyone wore poppies and at eleven o'clock a siren sounded as the signal for two minutes silence. Wherever a person might be at that time, at work, at home or in the street, they stopped what they were doing and paused to remember those who had sacrificed their lives. I remember very clearly seeing men dismount their bicycles, take off their caps and stand with heads bowed for that brief two minutes. Anyone who didn't observe the silence was considered disrespectful.

Sunday was the public remembrance day, when townspeople congregated on the market place to pay homage. There was always a very large crowd, the entire area between the butter cross and the war memorial being filled with people of all ages. Entire families converged on the market place from all over the town, then stood quietly waiting in the cold for the parade to arrive.

One could hear the band gradually approaching, followed by the marching of hundreds of feet as representatives of all local organisations came into view, arms swinging and heads erect for that most important of occasions. The Territorial Army unit usually followed the band, uniforms embellished by gleaming buttons and dazzling white webbing. Then came Girl Guides and Brownies, Boy Scouts and Wolf Cubs, the St. John Ambulance brigade and other units. But the most important participants in the parade were the war veterans, medals glinting on their chests, shoulders squared as they marched on their special day. Some limped from old wounds or had empty coat sleeves; others showed the disfigurement of primitive plastic surgery, but their gait and their bearing were military and their attention to the proceedings was undivided as they remembered fallen comrades.

When all members of the parade had gathered in the space allotted them around the war memorial, the service began, conducted by clergy from churches and chapels, bringing all denominations together on that poignant occasion. Poppy wreaths were laid by both individuals and representatives of groups and organisations. Everyone joined in prayers and the hymns that belong to that day. *O God Our Help In Ages Past* and *Eternal Father, Strong To Save* sounded both moving and stirring as the voices of the crowd rang out into the raw, damp November afternoon. The haunting notes of *The Last Post*, played by a lone trumpeter standing at the edge of the butter cross, echoed across the old market place, bringing tears and memories to many. Then a member of the clergy spoke the words we have come to know so well.

They shall not grow old as we that are left grow old; age shall not weary them, nor the years condemn. At the going down of the sun and in the morning, we will remember them.

Then the crowd quietly dispersed, each person returning home with his or her own special thoughts and memories.

* * * * *

SCHOOL DAYS

The Broad Street primary school was just over fifty years old when I enrolled there at the tail end of the 1920's. An attractive, solid Victorian building, it stands at the junction of Market Street and Broad Street; an adjoining house that was occupied by the headmaster is built in the same architectural style. Upon entering the wide gateway that led past the headmaster's back yard, two separate buildings came into view: one was for children up to seven years old, called *The Infants' School*; the other, known as *The Big School*, was for juniors aged seven to eleven. Both sections of the school were staffed by a dedicated group of teachers during the years I attended and I remember them with both affection and respect. A few spent their entire teaching careers at the school, while others taught there for only a brief period before moving on to other schools or to marry and raise their own families. Almost all were female; during the period I attended the school, only one teacher, apart from the headmaster, was male.

Of all those who taught during that period, the one who made the most lasting and vivid impression on me - and I'm sure on many other pupils - was Miss Cole, the headmistress of The Infants' School. I can see her as though it were yesterday, loping through the classrooms with her long, bouncy stride, strings of beads dangling and jangling as she paused to bend over a child's desk. She was tall, middle-aged, with greying hair and rimless eye-glasses attached to a cord worn around her neck. She seemed usually to wear black or dark-coloured dresses in the straight, shapeless style of that era, with the waistline, if it could be called such, around her hips. She had a sporty side too, being the owner of a car with a dickey seat in which she drove dashingly away after school each day, the engine coughing and spluttering as she zoomed off along Market Street to her home in a nearby village. This also gave her an air of mystery, as we never saw her when we were out shopping or walking with our parents, as we did the other teachers who lived in the town.

My first contact with Miss Cole came when my mother took me to the school one afternoon to ask if I might begin attending as I was almost five years old, could read a few words and count very well. I had also talked of nothing else for months. Miss Cole came out of the school to speak to us and after asking me a few questions and admiring my doll in its pram, told my mother I could begin school.

I set out that first day after the Easter holidays, nervous but excited, wearing a spanking new navy blue dress with a red velvet collar, black stockings and a white-dotted pink pinafore that tied in a bow on each side at the waist. The pinafore was to protect my new dress. Along with several other newcomers I joined what was known as *The Babies Class* and eagerly began my initiation into the academic world. After a few weeks in that first class I spent brief periods in two other classes before coming under the tutelage of Miss Cole herself.

I recall very little of those first weeks beyond repeating letters and practising numbers, except for one incident, still very clear in my mind. It seems both amusing and tragic in retrospect, but was very serious to we children at the time it occurred. It concerned a girl I will call Betty, though that wasn't her real name. On that particular day she shared my desk; our desks were actually low tables with chairs for two children at each. After prayers and before our morning lessons began that day, another girl in the classroom began waving her hand in the air to attract the teacher's attention; having done so, she stood up and with all the drama of a small girl with important news to impart said, "Please, Teacher, Betty hasn't got no knickers on."

The astonished stares of an entire class of prudish five year olds were turned on the unfortunate child sitting next to me. She hung her head with shame and embarrassment. Teacher walked along the aisle to her and asked if it were true. Betty, shivering in a thin dress though it was a winter day, nodded her head and began to cry. Teacher then asked her gently, "Do you have a warmer dress at home?" A shake of the head was Betty's reply.

Teacher took her by the hand, led her to the front of the class, then opened our classroom door to summon Miss Cole, who after a brief conference, took the weeping Betty home. She came from a family very much poorer than most and though I have no recollection of subsequent developments, I feel sure that underwear and warm clothing were found so that the little girl was able to return to school more adequately clad.

Once in Miss Cole's class our serious learning began. With her long ruler she tapped out letters written on the blackboard, teaching us the sounds and magically forming words from them. I still recall the wonder of how easy it was to read once the sounds of the letters had been learned. Miss Cole inspired in me and I'm sure in countless of my contemporaries, a love of reading that has never subsided. She often read stories and poems aloud to us, opening up a marvellous world of poetry and literature. One of her favourite poems was *Pippa's Song*. I could always imagine Pippa dancing through the early morning fields, dew still on the grass. The last line of the poem, *All's right with the world,* seemed somehow comforting and cosy; everything wasn't all right with the world at that time, any more than the world is all right now, but we were too young to know that.

One day we had to write in our books, at the beginning of the January term the date, month and the new year 1930. Miss Cole taught us the meaning of the word *decade*, which we'd never heard before; she told us we were beginning a new one and that the old decade had gone forever. Little did anyone know that by the end of that new decade the world would be a very different place indeed.

In those days, before the discovery and development of antibiotics and other drugs that are commonplace today, childhood diseases were often serious and sometimes fatal. If we contracted measles, mumps, chicken pox or other such illnesses we were obliged to stay away from school for several weeks and even our brothers and sisters were kept at home until it was established they had neither contracted the disease nor could infect others. It was possibly during a period of widespread infection, or perhaps while an epidemic of a specific disease was rampant, that Miss Cole attempted to wage a one-woman battle to try and prevent at least some of her pupils from becoming infected. Every morning before lessons began she produced a glass spray bottle, rather like a perfume spray, which it probably was; the bottle was filled with a fluid with which she sprayed the inside of each child's mouth. We sat, mouths open like baby birds in a nest as Miss Cole walked up and down the rows of desks and squirted a little of the liquid into each one. We were allowed to eat one sweet afterwards, if we didn't like the taste. I have no idea what the spray contained, but I do know that occasionally, when I open certain containers of medicinal, or even cleaning fluids some sixty years later, there is a component that assails my nostrils and carries me back to that classroom of the 1930's and a caring headmistress who vainly tried to prevent infectious diseases from spreading through her school. We caught them anyway, and subsequently missed weeks of lessons.

Miss Cole had a system of awarding coloured stars for excellence in work: green, red, blue and gold stars for spelling, sums, reading and writing and most pupils tried very hard to achieve that almost impossible goal of ten out of ten for each subject. Often, illness prevented it even if we had the ability to do good work or, as so often happened in my own case, one subject failed us each term. Mine was writing; it was bad then and I must admit, hasn't improved much since. However, I recall one term when I had obviously missed no time due to illness and must have been extra careful over my writing because pinned up on the classroom wall and shown on my report at the end of the term, were those forty stars, ten out of ten in each colour. It was heady excitement.

Miss Cole's reports were wonderful: after detailing our term's achievements on the letter-sized, thin sheets of paper, she wrote a paragraph that was an uncannily accurate summation of our potential. She assessed in those few lines of sharply-pointed handwriting our character and abilities and how she perceived our qualities - or lack of them - affecting our academic futures. She knew us very well, knew our family backgrounds and the type of encouragement or praise required in order to urge each child to try just a little harder.

I'm certain most of us did try to please her, but there were a few pupils who would never achieve their potential or who had no interest whatever in school or learning. I remember one boy of whom even Miss Cole must have despaired. He was the school's Bad Boy; dirty, sullen and lazy, dressed in clothes that were often torn, grubby and ill-fitting. His facial features were rather handsome in a brooding manner, his eyes dark and piercing. He appeared to hold a grudge against everyone, peers and teachers alike, an attitude probably due to his impoverished, socially unacceptable home background. He was sometimes moved from his regular classroom, where he often disrupted lessons, to sit under the eagle eye of Miss Cole, in her own room. It made little difference; he still pinched and kicked the boy or girl who sat beside him or caused other disruptions. He developed into a juvenile delinquent and an even more delinquent adult; he was sent to prison on several occasions for various types of crimes. I have often wondered what kind of an older man he turned into: I have no knowledge of whether he continued to commit crimes or whether he was eventually rehabilitated.

Every year the Broad Street School staged an evening's entertainment for the public, the Infants and Juniors each acting a play. It was an exciting occasion, involving weeks of preparation and rehearsals and was, I'm certain, Miss Cole's favourite time of year. Having chosen a play, one that gave scope to a large cast, pretty costumes and usually numerous fairies and elves, the principal actors were chosen. It wasn't only acting ability that counted: the principals were required to have a voice that would carry in a large hall, a good memory and regular attendance at school. The latter was imperative, as a child who was constantly ill or absent for other reasons could not be relied upon. Miss Cole's judgement was good and her plays, eagerly anticipated by parents, children and the general public, were always a great success.

Most afternoons when the day's lessons had been completed, desks were pushed aside, a screen dividing two classes folded back and the play was rehearsed. The leading characters repeated their lines until they were word perfect, fairies and elves practised their dances and everyone their exits and entrances. Professional actors could not have been more conscientious. Those children not taking part in the play watched, the understudies paying particular attention.

Miss Cole meanwhile, in her own time at home, began her annual task, which I feel certain was a labour of love, of making all the costumes for the play. I always imagined that her house must have looked a little like Santa's workshop at that time of year, strewn with rolls of coloured crepe paper, fine wire for fairy wings, shimmery gauze and reels of thread. I wouldn't have been at all surprised to know that elves sat with her, sewing costumes far into the night.

Each morning after sitting down at our desks, we glanced at Miss Cole's own desk to see if she had a parcel there, for as each costume was completed, she brought it to school wrapped in sheets of newspaper held together with dressmaker pins.

As each costume was made and brought to school, a pleasant little ritual was enacted. The child for whom the outfit was intended was led into the cloakroom, divested of his or her school garments, then shivering with cold and excitement, dressed in the latest creation of Miss Cole's needle. When the costume had been fitted to her satisfaction, she led the child by the hand through all the classrooms so that everyone in the school could see and admire the pretty, crepe paper costume. The fairy dresses were beautiful, blue for Fairy

Bluebell, yellow for Fairy Primrose and so on, each decorated with tiny paper flowers and with fragile, gauze wings attached at the back. When everyone had oohed and aahed and admired, the child changed back into every day clothes and the costume was re-wrapped in its protective newspaper until the day of the concert. They were stored in the classroom, hauled by a length of string, pulley-wise, to hang from ceiling beams, safe from crushing.

If those costumes had been made from silks and satins and adorned with jewels they could not have evoked more pleasure from either wearers or viewers. I'm sure Miss Cole was very aware that the little processions through the classrooms were a bright spot in what were sometimes drab days.

The year I was fortunate enough to be chosen to wear one of the pretty fairy dresses and speak a few lines I did, after all, let Miss Cole down by becoming ill and was unable to take part in the public performance. I recovered sufficiently to be taken to see the play, though I hadn't returned to school. I watched with interest the results of the hours of rehearsal in the classroom, but when a dark-haired little girl made her entrance wearing *my* Bluebell dress and speaking *my* lines I felt the pangs of jealousy and regret.

But my time did come. A year or two later, I played a leading comedy role in the Junior School play and savoured the headiness of making an audience laugh.

At seven years old we moved to the junior section of the school that up to that point we'd always referred to as *The Big School*. There was a great deal of trepidation concerning that major step, even though physically we were simply moving to classrooms only a few yards distant from our cosy, familiar building. I recall being particularly nervous as I'd been very ill that year and hadn't attended school at all after the beginning of March, so it was somewhat daunting to return to school in September to pick up the threads of education in an unknown environment with new teachers and a stern headmaster instead of our kind, protective Miss Cole.

Even entering the school on the first morning was a strange experience: until then we'd hung up our coats in the cloakroom, then lined up among the racks of coats before filing into classrooms. But to enter The Big School, each class lined up outside in the playground; we were pushed and coaxed into order by a teacher and then, just before classes were due to begin, there emanated from inside the school the sound of one of the teachers pounding out on an upright piano, the march that was to become so very familiar. *The Boys Of The Old Brigade.*

Steadily-y, shou-oulder to shoulder,
Steadily-y bla-ade by-y blade.
Steady and strong, marching along,
The boys of the old Brigade.

Exhorted by teachers to keep our shoulders back, chests out and to swing our arms, we strode into school every morning to the strains of that never-to-be-forgotten march.   On the occasions I've heard it played since then, I have been mentally transported back to the early 1930's, the chalk-smelling classrooms of the Broad Street Junior School and lines of children marching into them from doors at each end of the building.

J.P. McCarthy, the headmaster, was a stern-faced unsmiling man who bustled through the classrooms each morning in a business-like manner to confer with teachers before settling into his study to attend to administrative affairs.   He didn't regularly teach a class, but sometimes took over if a teacher was absent or if he was carrying out one of his periodic tests of our knowledge.

In his house that adjoined the school he lived with his large family, several of whom also became teachers.   The youngest of his children was in the same class as I was.   I recall one occasion on which the boy replied to his father's question by inadvertently calling him Dad. Mr. McCarthy curtly reminded his son that in the classroom he was to address his father as Sir.

However, Mr. McCarthy was basically a kindly man, concerned about his pupils, anxious to broaden their minds and to teach them as much as possible during the years he was responsible for their education.   His methods were disciplinary and old-fashioned, but they worked, and every child in that school had the opportunity to acquire a good grounding in the three R's as well as participating in physical education, drama, crafts, singing, folk dancing and other activities.

Those were the days of scholarships to academic secondary schools and only a few places, eagerly competed for, were made available each year.   As was customary in many junior schools of that era, a group of promising pupils was chosen from the lower classes in the school and placed with the top class, there to share many of the older children's lessons and to be coached to make a good showing in the annual scholarship examinations set by the county education authorities. In retrospect, I find myself disagreeing with that concept, despite the fact I was among the chosen pupils when I attended the school. The system gave false hope to many children, as only a very few would win a coveted scholarship; often only one or two girls each year were successful in gaining places at the high school in the nearby town of March and possibly half a dozen boys went on to the grammar school there. Today's methods of streaming may not be perfect, but a large number of children with academic ability are given the opportunity to develop their full potential and indeed, doors to higher education are open to anyone who has the desire, ability and motivation to pursue a scholastic career.

Our basic education followed the pattern of most schools during that era: each morning we recited multiplication tables in unison until we knew them by heart, up to the twelve times table. Do children today learn only up to the ten times now that the metric system is in use? Do they learn tables at all?

We were frequently tested in spelling and mental arithmetic, learned the rudiments of history and geography and wrote numerous essays; our minds became sharply honed, retaining information and clamouring for more. The skills we learned during those years carried us into our adult lives, preparing us well for whatever type of education, job or career we pursued.

There was also a lighter side of school life, when regular lessons could be set aside. We spent many happy summer afternoons outdoors, learning country dances set to age-old traditional tunes played on a gramophone that stood on a chair in the corner of the playground. We gave an annual display for the benefit of parents and friends, performing *Rufty-Tufty, Gathering Peascods* and other such well-known dances. We wore our best dresses and tried hard to remember all the steps.

One or two afternoons each week we spent time learning and singing English folk songs, vocalising them cheerfully and lustily, if not always tunefully. We made the rafters ring with *Johnny's So Long At The Fair, The Ashgrove, Early One Morning*, rollicking sea shanties and difficult songs like *The Last Rose Of Summer*, that we could never get quite right.

From the school library, actually a well-stocked bookcase, we could choose a book and just sit and read in periods that were called *Silent Reading*. I recall discovering a book of Andrew Lang's fairy tales one day and over the next few years, whenever the opportunity arose, I read them all. They were enchanting. I also had a passion at that time for stories about girls' boarding schools and longed to attend one to find out if the girls really did hold midnight feasts in the dorm and whether they were as jolly and friendly as the stories suggested.

Some afternoons we sewed, knitted or embroidered and learned other crafts, carrying out the tasks messily and untidily at times, but enjoying them immensely, especially such activities as *papier maché*. A few interested girls remained after lessons one afternoon each week to be taught the art of crochet by a teacher who volunteered her time; we persevered with the manipulation of the unfamiliar crochet hook and fashioned odd-looking berets that we seldom if ever wore, but I for one have been ever grateful for having learned that skill. I have spent many relaxing hours over the years crocheting household items, garments, blankets and toys.

Finally, we were ready to face the world of secondary school, to graduate to whatever type of school had been decreed for us either by academic ability or family status and income. Because I was one of the pupils fortunate enough to be awarded a scholarship to the girls' high school, my education in Whittlesey ended at the age of eleven, when I left the Broad Street school.

I shall always remember with warmth and affection my friends of those early years, the games we played, the topics we discussed, the boys we giggled over, our plans for ourselves. I remember the clothes we wore and the clothes we wished we could wear, the people we liked and disliked and our budding adolescence. Huddling in groups in the playground we discussed with awe the startling discoveries we were beginning to make about our bodies. One girl had read hair-raising accounts of sexual matters in her parents' medical book and imparted the details with relish, but we didn't believe such things could possibly be true. No one would behave in that manner, we argued. Our mothers didn't enlighten us either, at least most of them didn't, until the moment when it became unavoidable and then only the sketchiest of information was given to us.

Sex education in schools was a long way into the future, but we didn't feel the lack of it and despite our "hole and corner" initiation into the mysteries of life, we grew into normal adults and parents without impaired psyches, and apart from the small minority found in every generation, we were neither promiscuous nor inhibited.

After almost one hundred years of housing the town's primary school population, the Broad Street school stands bereft of pupils. Only the ghosts of children past glide through the classrooms. If you listen very carefully, you can hear them reciting multiplication tables or singing folk songs to the accompaniment of an old, upright piano, the same piano that provided the music to which we marched into school each morning. In the playground there are faint echoes of country dance tunes, girls chanting as they skip with ropes, boys whooping as they chase each other and the voices of teachers shouting instructions and encouragement to children playing team games.

Newer, larger, modern buildings house the present generation of primary-age children with their need for space and technical equipment we never dreamed of. There are those who see the old school as a Victorian relic and several years ago there was talk of its being demolished, but due to a public outcry, it was spared the wrecker's ball. For my part, I hope that no one who attended the school will ever see another building there, or even a vacant site.

The Broad Street school building has been given a face lift and a new lease of life as a billiards hall. Perhaps some former pupils now use the school building to while away an hour or two of their leisure time.

Half a world away, I have displayed in my home a commemorative mug, designed by a local artist and sold in hundreds when the school seemed doomed to destruction. A black and white representation of the school adorns the mug and like so many other former pupils, I regard it as a tangible reminder of my early school days and the happy years I spent learning the basics of education.

*****

SUNDAYS

Sunday has long been regarded as a day to relax and set aside the week's work. In past generations, people obeyed the words of the Bible: *Six days shalt thou labour, and do all thy work; but the seventh day is the Sabbath of The Lord thy God: in it thou shalt not do any work.* And further: *Remember the Sabbath day, to keep it holy.*

Far fewer people now celebrate Sunday as a holy day. It is still a day of relaxation, but with today's shorter work week and longer holidays, Sunday is seen not as a single day of respite, but rather as part of the weekend, a time in which to revitalise the mind and body for the week ahead. Life today is more comfortable than it used to be, yet also more complex and more competitive. There is a hankering to acquire possessions of the type that were far beyond the reach of our predecessors, often precipitating the need for higher incomes in order to pay for the new material wealth. This merry-go-round of money chasing goods chasing money has been a cause of marital and other problems in many families. With pressures in the work place added to world tensions, mental stress has increasingly replaced the bone-weariness of long hours of manual labour that was the lot of a significant segment of the population during my childhood.

Changing life styles have inevitably altered weekend customs. An outing to the seaside or country in the family car or a weekend trip with tent or caravan are commonplace. Clad in comfortable, casual attire, many families spend all or part of their weekends in activities such as camping, golfing, fishing, sailing, hiking and the like; or they putter about their homes and gardens, read, or indulge in other relaxing occupations. No longer do people don special Sunday outfits that are rarely worn at other times; in fact, few people own such clothes. Other acquisitions have replaced those dressy, restrictive Sunday garments as the status symbols they once were.

The Sundays of my childhood were very different and they stand out in my memory as set apart from other days of the week. As I grew older I discovered that many people, even then, did none of things we did on Sundays: they didn't attend church services or Sunday school, were allowed to play cards and other games, to knit and sew, and in fact they regarded Sunday as though it were a holiday but not a holy day. Sometimes I envied them their freedom from conformity, yet there was a sense of order and security in the customs and traditions that we, along with many other families, observed. The very rigidity of those childhood Sundays makes them a special memory.

Although as a young child I could not have expressed my feelings about our Sundays, or even have recognised that those feelings existed, I sensed that our traditional and disciplined Sabbaths were right and proper and that those who spent the day otherwise were missing a special experience. Later, when I began to break away from the rigidity, as much due to peer pressure as a real desire to do so, a sense of guilt tempered the pleasure of shaking off the proprieties, so ingrained were they in my thinking.

Sundays began differently from other days for almost everyone, because except on rare occasions, fathers were at home. Brickyard workers laid aside for that one day of the week their dust-impregnated clothing, farm labourers their mud-spattered overalls and others whatever was the working uniform of their trade or occupation. Instead, they donned clean, light-coloured shirts, Sunday suits or trousers and *low shoes* instead of the weekday work boots. No self-respecting labourer would think of wearing his working clothes on Sunday, it was considered disrespectful. The men got up late to a cooked breakfast of eggs and bacon or sausages and fried tomatoes instead of the hurried cup of tea and bread spread with whatever was available that constituted their weekday early morning meal.

I recall summer Sundays best, when after their leisurely breakfast, fathers took their digging forks and baskets and went off to their gardens or allotments to dig potatoes and pick peas, beans or green vegetables for the week's most important meal, Sunday dinner. The men had time to compare crops with neighbours and discuss gardening problems or perhaps walk along to another neighbour who kept a pig and join the men already leaning over the gate to admire the sty's porcine occupant as it rooted in the mud and straw. Conversation between the men was slow and spare in the fen tradition, but they understood each other perfectly, completely at ease in their Sunday morning companionship. This was *leisure* earned after a week of sweat in the brick kilns, exposure to weather in the farm fields, the noise of factories or days spent pleasing customers in local shops. Most people at that time worked a five and a half day week, therefore

Sunday was anticipated with pleasure and relished to the full when it arrived.

Sunday morning was for some men a time to visit their parents, who usually lived within cycling distance; older children often accompanied their fathers on their own bicycles, while a younger child rode on Dad's cross-bar seat.

About midday there was a migration to the pubs for a pint or two and a discussion of the week's sporting scene or the local crop situation; perhaps even a chance to expound on politics and local affairs. And although the men would never admit it, they liked a good old gossip about who in the town was doing what, and with whom. Then they mounted their bicycles and made their way home for a dinner of roast beef and Yorkshire pudding after which, sated, it was off to bed or a comfortable armchair for a long snooze.

Mother meanwhile, aided by daughters if they were old enough, had been busy heating up the Yorkshire pudding batter and making sure the coal range was stoked exactly right to heat the oven to the correct temperature for cooking the meat and pudding and perhaps also a tray of little cakes or tarts for tea. Father sometimes brought home a bottle of stout from the pub for Mother; then tired and hot from the morning's exertion and often from small children under her feet, she sat down to enjoy the cool, invigorating beverage while the vegetables cooked.

Afternoons were for Sunday school. As soon as the dinner table was cleared we, like many other children of neighbouring families, were dressed in carefully-ironed Sunday dresses, or Sunday suits for the boys. Shoes were polished to a mirror-like shine or in summer, whitened to a dazzling brightness. Girls completed their summer outfits with the detested straw hats that irritated one's ears beyond belief. With elastic under the chin to prevent their blowing off, those beribboned, flower-adorned hats were so pretty, but such a penance to wear. They were however, a traditional item of summer Sunday outfits and helped to make the day special. Even during those economically depressed years, there were very few children who did not have special clothing to wear on Sundays.

With children out of the way and the baby sleeping, Mother was able to get her feet up for an hour or so and settle down with the Sunday newspaper, a woman's magazine or a good book. We always returned far too soon for her liking: it seemed she'd barely begun to catch up on her reading when there we were, home again.

We weren't allowed to play noisy games outside, skip or play ball; card games were not allowed, neither could we knit or sew or busy ourselves with many activities that might have kept us quietly amused for a hour or two. Reading was approved of, which suited me, being a voracious reader and it was the one day of the week I was never reprimanded for *having my head stuck in a book* when I was supposed to be doing something else. I wallowed in *Grimm's Fairy Tales,* its bright blue cover battered by constant use, many of its pages loose with much turning. *Tanglewood Tales* was another favourite; my edition had vivid, coloured pictures of Jason and the Golden Fleece, Atlas supporting the world on his shoulders, Medusa of the snake-like hair and numerous other of the mythological characters of those tales. Some were rather fierce and scary in appearance, but that only added to their attraction for me. We also had the weekly edition of *Tiny Tots* to read, my favourite serial story strip being *Little Snowdrop,* a waif-like orphan. There were a few books saved from my mother's childhood, the best-remembered of those being *Uncle Tom's Cabin,* which I read two or three times.

But even reading had its limits: I read everything in sight, then complained there was nothing else to read. I began to write my own stories in a penny exercise book and wish now that some of them had survived. Today's children are so fortunate in their access to libraries. How I would have loved to borrow new books to read each week! At that time one was permitted to join our local public library at twelve years of age, there being no books available for young children. I longed to attain that magic age and go along to the senior boys' school where the books were set out on desks one evening each week and there, choose my own preferred books. The selection was not particularly inspiring, the same books appearing week after week, but there was always something suitable; or even unsuitable, but interesting. Eventually, a permanent library was opened, no longer restricted to one evening per week, but by that time I was a teenager and able to borrow books elsewhere, including my school library.

After returning from Sunday school I often watched from our front window for my grandparents to pass by on their way to the cemetery, where they placed fresh flowers on family graves. I sometimes joined them and was allowed to fill the watering can, empty the previous week's dead flowers and arrange the new ones. Then, like many others who had tended graves, we strolled around the cemetery at a sedate, Sunday pace to admire floral tributes on new graves and sometimes stop to read the attached cards. It was a perfectly acceptable thing to do, although in retrospect, it strikes me as rather an odd manner in which to pass a Sunday afternoon.

If it was too cold to go to the cemetery, we children still watched for our grandparents as they always called in to visit us on their way home to bring us a bag of sweets from their own shop, usually chocolate drops, jelly babies or dolly mixtures. We enjoyed their presence too: Grandma with her navy blue silky coat and straw hat in summer and dark, fitted coat with a fox fur draped around her shoulders in winter; and always a scent of perfume or of the parma violet cachous she sucked. In winter, she changed to Victory V lozenges, black, hot and strong, burning one's mouth. Grandpa had a military bearing, a waxed, curled moustache, black bowler hat, incredibly shiny boots or shoes and always carried either a silver-topped walking stick or a furled umbrella. He was merry and playful and had twinkling blue eyes.

Sunday teatime was special. The table was set with the china tea service my parents had received as a wedding present: delicate, china cups, saucers and tea plates, with sugar basin and milk jug to match, patterned with orange flowers. We thought it very pretty. One of my sisters now has the sole remaining item of that tea set. We ate thinly-cut bread and butter, jelly and blanc mange, followed perhaps by little cakes in paper cups, jam tarts or sometimes slices of buttered currant bread.

After tea on summer evenings we usually went for a walk, *en famille*. When we were older, we attended Evensong, but as young children we set off for a long walk. Country roads were closer to home in those days, before the post-war building boom appropriated farm land for houses. Once past the gypsy encampment - eyed very warily from a safe distance - we children raced ahead of our parents along the narrow, gravelled road that was already peopled by other families, mothers pushing prams and older children skipping along beside or ahead of them, the light, bright colours of their summer clothes as gay as the wild flowers that grew in profusion.

Ditches were filled with tall, white-blossomed cow parsley, known locally as *kek* and looked down on as the Cinderella of wild flowers. We never picked it. The grass verges on either side of the road were yellow with buttercups and celandines, with tiny, white, pink-tipped daisies nestling among them. In early summer the tall hedgerows were a mass of creamy-white, heavily-scented may blossom and wild rose bushes clung to the edges of ditches, their delicate, pale pink blooms protected by ferociously sharp thorns, making it almost impossible to gather them. Yarrow, vetches, stonecrops and the lowly dandelion grew prolifically, the scents of all the flowers mingling and filling the air with an unforgettable Sunday perfume.

We gathered large bunches of the flowers, never heeding our parents advice to pick them on the way home, to give them a chance to live, preferring to strangle the life from them in our hot little hands. Later, we placed them in jam jars on the kitchen window sill, but they soon wilted and died, unable to survive away from the life-giving earth where they belonged.

Occasionally, we walked as far as a marshy, enclosed area known as *The Pits*, where wild yellow irises grew among the bulrushes and where water lilies floated, serene and waxy as lotus flowers among their flat, fleshy leaves. Father climbed over the five-barred gate and ventured to the edge of the muddy marsh to pick a few irises, that he called *flags*. They lasted for several days in a tall vase and were very elegant.

Then we turned for home, tired, complaining of aching legs, thirst and hunger, our bunches of flowers wilting, our energy spent. The endless road no longer seemed a wild-flower garden to be explored, but a tortuous ordeal to be endured step by step, like a dream in which one never reaches one's destination. The sun sank lower and lower in that wide sky that met the horizon far beyond the flat fields of grain, sugar beet and potatoes, but it never quite disappeared before we reached home.

Finally arrived, we slumped into chairs and satisfied our hunger with thick slices of bread spread with dripping from the Sunday roast beef and drank water or lemonade or occasionally home-made ginger beer; we were ravenous after the exercise and fresh air. Soon packed off to bed, we slept easily, despite the indigestible food we'd eaten so quickly.

Those summer evenings, warm, still and scented, form an idyllic memory, a blend of wild flowers, summer dresses and simple pleasures. There must have been Sundays that were cool or wet or windy, but they are not remembered. Childhood almost always happened on sunny days.

On occasional Sundays during the summer, we visited our paternal grandparents who lived in the nearby village of Coates. I looked forward to those visits because their home was quite different from ours and from that of our other grandparents. Sometimes we cycled the few miles, on other occasions we travelled by bus. Although it was such a short distance away, it seemed another world. There was a village green with houses and small cottages clustered along each side, many of them since demolished. I was born in one of those cottages, though spent only the first year of my life there. One or two donkeys grazed on the green then and sometimes there were geese too, fierce in appearance and to be avoided.

We walked or cycled to the end of the green then turned on to a winding back road where stood our grandparents cottage, set to the rear of about an acre of land that was mostly cultivated. To one side of the cottage were a stable and other buildings and on the other, fruit trees and a large walnut tree, all affording ideal areas in which to play. Fascinating to us, water was hauled from a deep well, icy cold and clear; a pail of the well water always stood on a bench outside the kitchen door, with a wooden-handled dipper to drink from. Tea was laid in the long kitchen with a delicious selection of fruit, bread and farm butter, cakes and tarts. After tea, cousins, aunts and uncles arrived from their nearby homes and we played with our cousins in the long grass beneath the plum and apple trees and often gave ourselves stomach cramps from eating too much of the fallen fruit. Grown-ups sat beside the rose garden outside the front door on benches and chairs and talked. My grandfather sometimes allowed us to peer through his binoculars at distant bridges, trains and buildings that with the naked eye were simply dots on the horizon. A few years later, when I travelled by train to school every day, I used to look for my grandparents' house from the train window.

On several Sunday evenings during the summer months the town band gave concerts, always in the gardens of one of the large houses owned by local professional or other affluent residents. Those people generously opened up their grounds to the public on such occasions. One garden I recall very well: the band played on an expanse of lawn behind the house, the lawn sloping down to formal flower beds, rose-covered trellises and narrow gravelled paths from which one could admire the floral displays and the shrubs and trees that surrounded the garden.

The concerts commenced about eight o'clock, to allow those who had attended evening church services to get there in time. The audience meandered along roads that led to the gardens: families with children, young and elderly couples and a sprinkling of adolescents, all admiring the neat front gardens of houses along the route. Once arrived at the concert site, most settled themselves for the evening's entertainment, sitting or standing behind the circle of bandsmen, while others strolled around the garden as they waited for the music to begin.

The concert almost always began with a rousing march, probably by Sousa. Perspiring in their thick uniforms that were too warm for a summer evening, the bandsmen valiantly blew and puffed away as children jumped up and down to the stirring sounds of the brass and older people tapped their feet. Later in the program, a perennial favourite, *In A Monastery Garden* was almost always played; the bell-like sounds from the percussion instruments and the gentle tune remain an abiding memory of those Sunday concerts and lovely gardens.

When children became bored and restless, they rolled down the grassy slope of the lawn; adolescent girls strolled arm-in-arm through the rose bowers, giggling as they eyed groups of the opposite sex, feigning surprise when they encountered the boys they had in reality been either following or scheming to meet face to face.

As twilight began to envelop the scene, lights shone from the open windows of the house on to the band, glinting on their instruments. The final number was played, often *Abide With Me*, after which the musicians folded their music, mopped their brows, unbuttoned their tunics and looked forward to a long, cool drink. Tired children were rounded up and a straggling line of families wended its way back to the town centre. The *Band In The Gardens*, as we called it, was over for another Sunday.

When we were considered old enough, my sister and I attended

Evensong, the younger children still being taken for walks after tea. The town seemed different on Sunday evening as we walked past closed shops along half-deserted streets. The Salvation Army was beginning its service on the market place and a few people stood watching or listening. Sometimes we accompanied our grandparents to church. Grandfather was a church warden and choir member, and as we crossed the market place a Salvation Army member walked over to collect the generous coin my grandfather always donated. He had served in the Great War and supported the Salvation Army ever afterwards.

At times we went to church reluctantly: summer evenings offered outdoor attractions and winter evenings a book by the fire. But once inside the centuries-old church the peace, the familiar hymns and prayers and the traditions drew one into the ancient liturgy that has continued for countless generations beneath the pillars and beams and gargoyles, and memorials to past parishioners and heroes. The services were especially moving and joyful at Easter, Christmas and other seasonal festivals, the lessons, anthems and hymns returning each year like old friends.

My own favourite festival was Harvest Thanksgiving. Even more so than at Christmas, the church was filled to capacity for the evening service and regular parishioners arrived early to ensure seats in their favourite pews. I went early because I liked to see others arrive; I was always an inveterate people-watcher. Entire families of farmers, smallholders and their employees crowded into the church, their tanned, weather-beaten complexions glowing above the unfamiliar best suits and ties, their long, country strides moving quickly along the aisles. Though they may perhaps have felt more at ease behind a plough or leading a team of horses than seated in a church pew, they would not have missed the one special Sunday each year that was theirs above all others, the Sunday they offered thanks for their garnered harvests.

The deep, stone sills beneath the arched windows displayed produce from parishioners' gardens; humble vegetables lay beside flowers and ears of wheat, while bronze and yellow chrysanthemums reflected the colours of autumn. Flowers bedecked the choir stalls and a large cluster of dusky purple grapes hung at the pulpit. Beside the lectern a loaf of bread in the form of a sheaf of wheat symbolised harvests everywhere. The bread of life, the basic food of man.

When the introductory notes of the processional hymn were played on the organ, the choir emerged from the vestry and the congregation rose to its feet. With a resounding voice the people poured forth their thanks for a successful harvest:

Come, ye thankful people, come,
Raise the song of harvest-home;
All is safely gathered in,
Ere the winter storms begin.

Children had their own harvest festival service in the afternoon. They took fruit, flowers and eggs that were laid at the chancel steps during the traditional hymn, *All Things Bright And Beautiful*, sung as the children walked from their pews to present their gifts, which were later donated to the hospital in Peterborough, mostly to children's wards.

Not everyone belonged to the Church of England. There were several non-conformist churches and chapels in the town during those years; Methodist, Baptist and others and many of our friends attended them. They held annual celebrations known as *anniversaries*, most of them at about the same time of year, so that for several weeks during early summer, each chapel in turn had its anniversary. The Sunday school children took part in a concert, reciting verses or singing, both in choruses and choirs or performing solos. Sometimes we accompanied friends to those Sunday anniversary celebrations and I recall the almost jolly atmosphere of them after the more solemn services held in our own church. Those taking part in the performance sat on a stage in front of the congregation, the children dressed in their Sunday clothes, often having new outfits for the occasion. The factor that most puzzled and intrigued me at those services was that at some chapels, laymen from the congregation rose and led the prayers and on occasion, even preached sermons. It appeared unorthodox indeed to a child raised in the C. of E. tradition. However, I also found it interesting and enjoyable, being always open to new experiences.

Later on Sunday evenings, Market Street, so quiet and almost deserted earlier, came to life with crowds of youths and adolescent girls. They were not then known as teenagers, we didn't use that term. Johnson's sweet shop was open and doing a brisk business; groups of youths gathered both inside and outside the shop as though it were a social club. It *was* an unofficial one. Other groups congregated at intervals along both sides of the street. There was really little else for them to do on a Sunday evening, but it was all very good-natured and high-spirited, with a lot of what was called *larking about*. In winter the youths gathered beneath street lamps, laughing and talking in the pools of light. Girls walked up and down the street, arm-in-arm with best friends, giggling and eyeing the boys, both sexes making chaffing, provocative comments, often self-consciously, but at the same time with bravado, spurred by the encouragement of companions. They would never have been so bold when alone! Occasionally a boy and girl paired off amid teasing wisecracks from friends and set off together for a walk, perhaps around *The Bower*, a path that wound beside a river bank, among trees and shrubs, with seats placed at strategic intervals along the way.

During the summer, Sunday excursions were often arranged either by bus or train to seaside resorts and some residents took advantage of the trips to take a break from the weekday world, if they could afford to do so. Many families were unable to afford such a luxury and for their children, the only day they went to the seaside was on the annual Sunday school outing. It was such an event for many of us that I have described it in detail in another chapter.

There are, I'm certain, some people who never experienced the type of Sundays we knew as children. I cannot speak for them. Sundays for us were disciplined, but pleasantly so for the most part and are remembered forever in a *mélange* of Sunday school and church, Yorkshire pudding, itchy straw hats, silky dresses, church bells, brass bands, special teas and warm, sunny days perfumed by wild flowers.

* * * * *

THE DOMESTIC SCENE

When we awake on a winter morning we reach out to switch on an electric light and perhaps a radio too, to listen to music or the news while we snatch an extra few minutes in bed. Then our feet swing out on to a warm rug and off we go to a bathroom where both hot and cold water for our morning ablutions gush forth at the turn of a tap. The toilet is flushed by gallons of water simply by pressing a lever.

Once dressed, or wearing a cosy dressing gown we make our way to a warm kitchen; if it's a very cold morning we turn up the thermostat or switch on a gas or electric heater. An electric kettle is filled and plugged in or a kettle is placed on a gas or electric burner. If we are coffee drinkers a coffee maker is plugged in. While the tea or coffee brews, we put out boxes of cereal bought from a wide selection at the local supermarket, then take milk, butter, marmalade or jam and perhaps orange juice from a refrigerator. Slices of bread from a packaged loaf are placed in an automatic toaster, Presto! Breakfast is ready, in just a few minutes.

Breakfast dishes are either washed right away with instant hot water or placed in a dishwasher to be attended to later in the day. Dressing and prework toilets completed, it's off to work in the family car or by public transportation located conveniently close to home. Children set out for school, well-fed usually and Mother either goes off to work herself or relaxes with another cup of coffee and the morning newspaper, unless she has pre-school children, in which case her daily chores will leave little time for relaxation for the following few hours.

My generation of children awoke in icy cold bedrooms on winter mornings, with flickering candlelight or perhaps a small oil lamp to provide illumination if it was not yet daylight. After several minutes of steeling ourselves to throw off the blankets, we emerged shivering into the chilly air and usually dashed downstairs in our night wear to warm ourselves by the fire that was already burning cheerfully in the big coal range. Hands and faces were washed in a bowl at the kitchen sink, cold water being warmed up a bit from a kettle of water heated on the fire. A visit to the privy meant dashing outside, wearing a coat if the weather was very cold. Then it was back to the fire, to warm up again and get dressed before breakfast.

Before we could do any of those things however, someone had performed many other chores before we were even awake. Usually it was Mother who came down wearing a coat or cardigan over her nightie to a chilled, cheerless room with the remains of yesterday's fire still in the grate. If it was still dark, she lit a lamp, raked out ashes from the grate, then placed them in a container to be sieved for burnable cinders. Then with newspaper and kindling she started a fire. As soon as it was burning she filled a kettle with just enough water to make a cup of tea and placed it over the burning wood. Tea made, she added coal to the sticks and soon had a roaring fire blazing, sitting to savour its warmth while she drank her well-deserved tea. The range was brushed and tidied and more coal added so there would be a glowing, red fire to make toast for breakfast. After a wash in the kitchen, she dressed by the fire before awaking the children. Father would have gone to work hours before. The big, iron kettle had been re-filled after making the tea and placed over the fire so there would be hot water for the children to wash themselves.

The lack of a bathroom, common in many working class homes of that period, caused problems. But everyone coped. Hands and faces were washed at the kitchen sink and more private washes took place at a wash stand in the bedroom, or one waited until the kitchen wasn't likely to be in use. Babies and small children were bathed before the fire in winter, in a galvanised bath filled from kettles boiled on the coal range; in summer they were bathed in the kitchen, often in the kitchen sink. The rest of the family bathed in a long, portable, galvanised tin bath that was hauled to wherever privacy could be found; a shut-off kitchen, an outdoor wash house or shed in summer, or in front of the fire in winter, after everyone else had gone to bed. Water for bathing was often heated in a built-in copper also used for wash days, the water being carried to the bath tub in pails. Bath water was shared; the luxury of fresh water for each person was next to impossible, especially in large families.

Although some families did have water laid on to an indoor tap over the sink, many still obtained their water from an outdoor pump that sometimes froze in winter and I recall that our family did so for a few years. This added an additional chore to wash days and bath nights. Rain water was used when possible, having been collected in a large, metal tank with a tap near the bottom to facilitate filling pails.

It was soft and silky for washing one's hair or body and very little soap or shampoo was required to whip up frothy suds. The supply of soft water depended of course, on the amount of rainfall and in very dry periods, the tank emptied. It was then given a good clean-out, an opportunity to get rid of insects and other flotsam that had managed to get into the tank.

But to return to winter mornings: after dressing by the fire we sat down to breakfast that was porridge, cereal or toast. Toast was made from slices of good, fresh bread cut from crusty loaves and held in front of glowing, red coals on the end of a long-handled, wire toasting fork. Striped in light and dark brown by the bars of the grate, then well-buttered, it was the best-tasting toast in the world, impossible ever to reproduce again.

Ready-to-eat cereals were beginning to make their appearance on breakfast tables at that time, though there were very few varieties from which to choose. A favourite was *Force*, rather like corn flakes and made popular by *Sunny Jim*, an advertising character depicted on the package. He was a smartly-dressed fellow, wearing a top hat, striped trousers and a tail coat; he had a long, thin protuberance at the back of his head, below his hat. We called it his brain. By saving *Force* box-tops, a *Sunny Jim* doll could be obtained and we had one eventually, after eating lots of *Force* and collecting box-tops from other people who didn't want a doll. Eating the cereal was supposed to make one full of vitality and when Radio Luxembourg gave us our first taste of commercial radio, *Force* was advertised over the air waves by a jingle about *Sunny Jim:*

High o'er the fence leaps Sunny Jim,
Force is the food that raises him.

Women of today, with for the most part, small families, often hold down jobs as well as being housewives and mothers. Appliances such as automatic washers, dryers and dish washers, clothing made from easy-care fabrics, supermarkets for ease of shopping, frozen and other convenience foods, deep freezers, cars, and houses that are built with labour-saving devices have all made it much easier for married women to work. On the other hand, many find themselves in a situation where they must work in order to pay for the modern conveniences that allow them to work. A vicious circle! But with laundry that takes care of itself, little ironing to do, meals that cook in a jiffy, shopping that can be done in a one-stop supermarket, why not work? Even in today's comparatively affluent society, many families are unable to afford luxuries, or even an annual holiday without a second income.

Few of our mothers worked regularly and those with large families almost never did so. In our local agricultural society women were needed for seasonal work and some mothers made extra money that way, to purchase additional comforts or luxuries, or just to make life financially a little easier. Those women usually worked from early morning until early afternoon, when they arrived home to finish their housework and set about cooking the evening meal for their families. It was not an easy life.

Mothers who stayed at home all day had plenty to do too. Often, they had a baby; babies arrived regularly in some families and once the older children had left for school and essential early morning chores had been completed, the baby had to be bathed and fed.

Infants wore cumbersome clothing in those days. For the first few weeks of their lives they were swaddled in long garments, though not perhaps as heavily as in previous generations. Almost always they wore the mandatory woollen vest, a cloth or towelling napkin with perhaps a second one pinned around them to soak up some of the wetness; then a long flannel garment that went around the body under the arms, rather like a wrap-over skirt, fastened by tapes that slotted through holes and then were tied at the back; sometimes a long petticoat was worn, cotton or flannel according to season; a long gown and woollen jacket topped off the baby's outfit, with often a small blanket wrapped around as well, to keep everything in place and provide additional warmth.

There was a ritual known as *shortening* a baby: this didn't involve cutting off part of its legs! It was the transition from long gowns to dresses and the elimination during the day of soaking wet long clothing. From then on, the baby wore soaking wet short dresses! Plastic pants were unknown, in fact plastic material was unknown and the available rubber pants were considered bad for baby's delicate skin, therefore were rarely used. A few mothers, considered old-fashioned by some, kept their babies in long garments beyond the acceptable period of time and I recall my mother disagreeing with that custom; she was very up-to-date and practical in her outlook and shortened her babies as soon as possible. There were none of the convenient, warm, freedom-giving, all-in-one stretchy garments that modern babies so cosily and comfortably wear. Once short clothes were worn, babies were dressed in woollen leggings with feet, often hand-knitted; houses were colder then and babies needed to be dressed more warmly than is necessary today. With the baby bathed, fed and put down to sleep, often in its pram outdoors, mother began to tackle the housework.

First, to save the bright, more expensive coal, she banked up the fire with coal dust and cinders to make it last all morning; by the time the children arrived home from school at dinner time it would be glowing red again and giving out a good heat. In summer, the fire would be allowed to die out after breakfast, being lit again only to provide sufficient heat to cook a meal later in the day. We eventually had a gas cooker installed in the kitchen, also a gas light in the living room, though we still used candles or lamps in the kitchen and bedrooms. It then became unnecessary to light a fire at all on summer mornings; the tea kettle was boiled on a gas burner and meals cooked by gas too, but the coal range was used for cooking in winter. Gas cost pennies in the meter and was used sparingly. The gas light too, was not lit until it was too dark to see without it. Tasks that required a good light were either completed during daylight hours or after the gas light was lit. A cosy living room, lit only by flames from a fire was not something to be dispelled unnecessarily by artificial light, but was a pleasure to be savoured; we liked to sit and look for pictures in the fire during the time between daylight and darkness. It was a time of day I recall with nostalgia.

But back to housework! Few working class families owned a vacuum cleaner, or carpets on which to use one for that matter. Hearth rugs were lifted each day and given a good shake outside, the linoleum-covered floors swept, shelves and ledges cleaned of the day's accumulation of dust, and bedrooms and other areas tidied and dusted. The house was quickly clean and cosy again. Each room was given a thorough weekly clean, one day devoted to ironing and mending, a time-consuming chore in those days, as was wash day. We enjoyed the day our mother polished the linoleum: she often did that on Saturday morning and when she had rubbed on a coating of *Mansion polish*, she allowed us to put old woollen socks on our feet and play at "skating", polishing the floor as we did so. We had fun and the floor was polished. Amazingly, we never did hurt ourselves.

The coal range received its weekly black-leading on Saturday mornings too, usually before we were up and about; every day it was brushed and tidied, but on Saturdays it was thoroughly cleaned and shined with brushes dipped in black-lead; the brushes, flat with handles on top, were wielded with a great deal of *elbow grease* to achieve the lustre that reflected fire light on its gleaming surface and would last the remainder of the week.

By the time the daily chores were completed, it was almost time to cook dinner for us. During the week, fathers were not often home for the midday meal, but we children usually had our big meal of the day at that time and we were starving after a morning at school. There were always potatoes and vegetables with a small helping of meat, cheese or occasionally, fish; good, filling currant or jam suet rolls, baked milk puddings or fruit-filled suet puddings in season. There were no frozen foods and in most families, meals were cooked from scratch, using basic, wholesome ingredients. Apart from some tinned goods, the only convenience food was fish and chips, but in large families that was a luxury, to be bought only occasionally. Vegetables were almost always home-grown and when that supply was exhausted we bought them from a greengrocer who came around once each week. Great ingenuity was required to feed a large family with meals that supplied the daily nutrients needed to maintain both health and gastronomic satisfaction. Our food was plain but nourishing, with few luxuries. There were no home freezers in which to store surplus fruit and vegetables for the winter, though whenever possible fruit was preserved in jars and jam was made from damaged fruit and blackberries picked from the hedgerows. We enjoyed fruit when it was in season and when it wasn't, we went without.

For most women it was a matter of pride to complete their cleaning chores before dinner time, except on wash day, which was a day-long operation. Afternoons were for shopping, mending, ironing, sewing, visiting and any of the more pleasant household tasks. Since no one owned a refrigerator, shopping was done frequently, often daily, which also provided an opportunity to take the children for a walk, perhaps meet other mothers and stop for a chat to talk over news and problems. Many people had accounts with tradesmen, obtaining the items they needed each day, then once a week, usually on Saturday, after Father had been paid, they settled their account for the shopthings they'd had during the week. The word *shopthings* pops into my mind quite naturally in thinking of that era, though I probably haven't heard it used for many years. It was a common expression that encompassed household supplies and food, usually those bought from the grocer.

The weekly wash was a major production, beginning early and lasting, in large families, well into the afternoon. Washing machines were in their infancy and few owned one. I never saw one during my entire childhood. The most important wash day aid was the boiler or copper. Some families owned gas or electrically-operated boilers, but in most homes a built-in copper stood in a corner of the kitchen or in an outside wash house. Made of cast iron, the copper was built into a brick surround with a fire grate underneath to heat the water. A heavy, wooden lid was placed over the copper during the boiling operation and turned upside down, it formed a flat surface on which to drain the items as they were fished out of the boiling, soapy water.

In order to get a good start to the day, mother rose extra early to fill the copper with water and light the fire under it so that hot water would be available as soon as she was ready to make a start on the piles of laundry. She may have soaked some of the wash overnight to ease the scrubbing time, but she still had a hard day ahead, interrupted by getting children off to school and perhaps attending to a baby in addition to numerous other tasks that required her attention during the day.

Washing equipment comprised a deep tub with a rim to prevent water splashing out, dolly pegs with which to swish the clothes around in the tub, galvanised baths or tubs for rinsing and bluing, a large bowl of starch mixture and strong wooden tongs or a stout stick to lift items from the copper after they had bubbled to a snowy whiteness. Hot water was baled from the copper into the tub and the first batch of laundry, usually white items, was agitated in a back and forth motion to release as much of the soil and as many stains as possible. Even then, some things had to be scrubbed by hand or on a wash board. With the "whites" boiling away and a satisfying cloud of steam issuing from wash house or kitchen into the early morning air, the next batch was attacked. Coloured and non-boilable items had to be hand-washed, scrubbed or pounded clean with dolly pegs, that acted rather like a hand-operated washing machine. It resembled a low, three-legged stool with a pole attached through the centre and a short handle across the top to be gripped as it was twisted back and forth. Muscles, strength and sheer stamina were required to move a tub full of laundry, especially large items such as sheets, table cloths or work clothing.

After the washing and boiling, everything had to be rinsed, then rinsed again in water with bluing added, in order to achieve that whiter than white appearance; cotton items and most household linens were starched to give them a crisp, professional finish when ironed. Before being piled in the wicker clothes basket to hang on the line, the entire wash was carefully folded to avoid unnecessary creases, then squeezed through the mangle's wooden rollers. The mangle was an important item of equipment and unless one had an outside wash house it stood in the kitchen or scullery all the time, large, cumbersome and often in the way. The rollers were built into an iron frame; it was operated by turning a handle at the side, pressing out surplus water and smoothing the garments at the same time.

On a fine, sunny day, with laundry billowing and blowing in the breeze, wash day could be almost a pleasure, but in winter and on wet days at any time of the year, it was a disaster. Wet clothes hung in the kitchen to dry, or steamed around the fire, much to the disgruntlement of family members who wanted to huddle around the fire themselves. On frosty days, washing came off the line frozen stiff and we laughed uproariously at underwear and shirts standing up by themselves.

When the washing was finally dry it was folded carefully and smoothly to facilitate ironing; starched items often had to be dampened again, as they invariably became too dry. Sheets, towels and other linens were once again rolled through the mangle after being folded, to avoid ironing them at all. I recall having to stand and *turn the mangle* after tea on wash day, while my mother fed items through the rollers, the pressure tightened to the limit, the better to press them. The huge pile of ironing was usually left until the following day, being a major chore in itself.

When the laundry was completed, usually by mid-afternoon, advantage was taken of the copper of hot, soapy water remaining from the final boiling of the day and everything in sight was scrubbed: table, kitchen floor, doorstep, outside drain, toilet etc., so that by tea time, poor mother was exhausted.

That same wash day ritual persisted into the early married years of many of my generation. No appliances were manufactured during the war years or the period immediately following the war, so we too, rose early on wash days to get the boiler going or light copper fires and wash the way our mothers did, without the benefit of washing machines. I and my contemporaries appreciate, as no young person ever can, the difference that washers and dryers have made to wash days. We don't even need to have set wash days. And too, we enjoy the freedom from ironing that easy-care fabrics have given us; not for today's young people the hours of ironing with flat irons to smooth out starched linens, shirt collars and frilly dresses as our mothers did, for even the minimum ironing necessary is done with steam irons that glide over material, miraculously removing wrinkles with very little pressure.

My mother's generation heated flat irons on the coal range or gas burners, one in use, another heating up, spitting on them to test the heat before pressing away on one end of the big, wooden table in the living room, on layers of old sheets and blankets. The not unpleasant smell of scorching and steam pervaded the room as clothes airers were draped with beautifully-ironed clothing, the pile in the wicker basket gradually diminishing. Ironing was a work of art: I loved to watch my mother, she did it so quickly and deftly and as each item was completed it looked like new. I have often wished she could have had the ease of modern laundry aids. When I recall the back-breaking wash days of our childhood I have great admiration for those mothers who accepted it as their lot and cheerfully tackled mountains of washing and ironing with almost primitive equipment and who, on warm, summer days when the laundry basket was piled with dry, sweet-smelling linen, felt that life was good to them.

Spring cleaning provided a break from the usual routine, gave the house a face lift and housewives a lift in spirit. They spent so much time in the house, cleaning, washing, cooking and caring for children, that a change of wallpaper and paint was as good as a change of scenery.

Most years, along with many other families, we re-papered the living room walls. We enjoyed that, as we all had a hand in it. First we borrowed a book of wallpaper samples from the shop that sold decorating supplies and spent an evening poring over it to decide whether we would have large leaves on a cool, green background, roses climbing over trellises or an *avant-garde* abstract design to form the backdrop of our domestic life for the following year. Then a border had to be chosen, for no room was complete without one, either neat and narrow or more elaborate and floral to decorate the top of the wall and hide the spots where the paper hadn't fitted properly below the picture rail.

Then came the part we children enjoyed most: stripping off the old wallpaper. It was gratifyingly destructive as well as fun and all with parental approval. The old paper was well soaked with warm water, then we had contests to see who could pull the longest piece of paper off the wall. We ended up ankle-deep in paper and border strips and when the mess was cleared away we could even draw or write our names on the wall.

Ornaments and pictures had been removed and stored safely in the front room. Ornaments were very popular then, though we had very few compared with some families; our mother didn't like what she referred to as *clutter*. Antimacassars, doilies and collections of dust-catching little pieces of china were not for her; for the most part, our decor consisted of a few items that had been received as wedding gifts or brought from places visited by family members, as well as a minimum of pictures and portraits.

Before any cleaning could begin, the chimney had to be swept. Every spring, chimney sweeps were kept busy from very early morning hours, removing the winter's accumulation of soot. They were a familiar sight in their black clothing with hands and faces to match, as they went from house to house, plying their trade. Some people swept their own chimneys, either buying or borrowing the equipment, adding one by one the extension rods that pushed the flat brush out of the chimney pot. The tricky part was collecting the soot to contain it in the grate, preventing it from settling on every ledge and surface in the room.

The first cleaning task was to whitewash the ceiling; smoke from coal fires and the oil lamp discoloured the ceiling over the winter months. We were unable to buy a tin of white paint for the ceiling; emulsion and latex paints hadn't been invented. To mix whitewash, a lump of whitening was purchased; it was rather like chalk in texture and in the shape of a large, fat sausage. It was pounded to a powder in a pail of water and stirred until the mixture was smooth enough to use.

With the ceiling restored to a snowy whiteness, the wallpapering was tackled. A paste was made with flour and boiling water and as each length was cut, we applied the thick, warm paste with a wide brush. As each wall was completed it was admired and when all four walls were finished and the border added it seemed we were living in a new home.

The next day we helped to clean the pictures and family portraits; Landseer's *Stag At Bay* and *Monarch Of The Glen* looked down at us through gleaming glass from shiny polished frames, their haughty expressions implying they really belonged in a far more elegant setting than that in which they found themselves. When we were old enough, we helped to wash the china items in warm, soapy water, then rinse and dry them. My favourites were the King Charles' spaniels with their tiny, squashed-up faces and painted chains, one silver, the other gold. They were part of my life from the very beginning, looking at me from sideboard, window sill or shelf. They are still a part of my life, having been carefully transported across the Atlantic to grace my present home, a perpetual reminder of my parents, my childhood and those far-off spring-cleaning days. The striking clock was re-hung in its accustomed place on the wall; furniture was polished and lace curtains washed, ironed and hung at the windows. A new, green felt mantel border with gold embroidery squiggling across the bottom was tacked in place to hang around the shelf above the fireplace and a new hearth rug, made during the long winter evenings, was laid before the fire. After tea, when the green plush tablecloth covered the big table and the lamp was placed on it, casting soft shadows around the room, we were enveloped in an incomparable warmth and cosiness.

In turn, the remainder of the house was turned upside down and thoroughly cleaned, room by room. Bedroom walls were often painted; we called it distempering, the green, blue, pink or beige colour washes produced by dissolving distemper powder in water, a lighter shade being obtained by adding a little whitewash.

Finally, we were totally spring-cleaned and ready to face another year. No family in a stately home with luxurious carpets, antique furniture, and old masters on the walls, could have been more satisfied than we hard-working families with our clean-smelling, face-lifted, modest homes.

The domestic scene in the 1920's and 30's, as in any age, encompassed far more than cooking, cleaning and daily child care. Our mothers, like mothers in all preceding generations, nursed their offspring through childhood diseases that could, and occasionally did result in death, however devoted and tireless their nursing skills.

Our childhood, the end of an era in so many aspects of life, also saw the end of interminable weeks spent in bed in isolated bedrooms to recover from measles, chicken pox, scarlet fever, whooping cough and other infections. Apart from a smallpox vaccination shortly after birth, most children did not receive immunisation against diseases as they do today. The more grave illnesses, such as diphtheria and tuberculosis were still prevalent; colds and influenza more quickly developed into pneumonia due to a lack of effective antibiotics; measles left many children with eye or kidney problems or other debilities and lack of sanitary facilities in some homes led to more easily-contracted infections. Poverty caused by economic depression was responsible in some cases for poor nutrition and lack of hygiene, sometimes resulting in contagious skin diseases; and doctors had fewer drugs at their disposal with which to fight the illnesses that plagued so many. There were some families too, who declined to call in a doctor until the patient was extremely ill, as they were unable to pay for his services or for prescribed medicines.

These and other causes resulted in lengthy and sometimes severe illnesses and if one child in a family contracted a disease, the rest had to stay home from school until it was ascertained whether or not they would succumb, in order to prevent the spread of infection. It didn't really help; epidemics raged and once a disease gripped a town or village, it spread to many families. Some children recovered rapidly, others suffered serious attacks, while a few never recovered. A great deal of time was missed at school, some children returning after an illness only to become infected with something else almost immediately, forcing them to begin the process all over again. Our mother, like some other parents, carried lessons back and forth from our teachers in an effort to keep us abreast of the class curriculum.

Home remedies were very popular, as they'd been for centuries, to combat and prevent illness and infection. Even families who could afford the regular services of a doctor used them as supplementary preventions and cures. There was a psychological effect too, in time-worn remedies, though we'd probably never heard of psychology. Remedies passed down from generation to generation often worked because we *believed* they would.

Hot bread poultices were applied to boils and other such infections to draw out poison, bringing many a scream from a luckless victim as a hot concoction, wrapped in a piece of clean white cloth was slapped on to the infected area. I recall a particular instance of such drastic treatment when I stepped barefoot on a rusty nail. A hot bread poultice on the sole of the foot was akin to mediaeval torture to an eight-year-old. Mustard baths or mustard plasters were prescribed for colds and chest complaints, as was rubbing the chest with camphorated or eucalyptus oil, or a mixture of the two. Country people often used goose fat for the same purpose and swore by its healing powers.

Medicines prescribed by doctors were sometimes little more than coloured water containing plenty of iron. Many people are able to recall being dosed with Scott's Emulsion, cod liver oil and malt, California syrup of figs and so on; I also remember sucking large sulphur lozenges, acid-yellow in colour and usually given during spring time to "clear our system".

For more serious illnesses, most families did indeed call in a doctor, even though it might take months to pay the fee, little by little. In retrospect, the doctor was a regular visitor to our house; there always seemed to be someone ill, often myself. The worst illness was diphtheria. During a serious epidemic of the disease, I only just survived that painful and frightening illness. A memory I recall from that time had nothing to do with the illness itself. On the day of my seventh birthday, when I was beginning to recover, a national census was held, and because it was my birthday, the doctor promised I could be carried downstairs from the bedroom in which I'd been confined for several weeks. After my younger brother and sisters were in bed, my father wrapped me in a blanket, carried me down and sat me in an armchair by the fire. It was a Sunday, and while he sat at the table filling out the census form, I precociously spelled out everyone's name, age and birthdate for him.

With our present health care system and its widespread services, drugs that were undreamed of fifty years ago, new methods of prevention of disease, well-nourished children and houses that for the most part are appointed with modern equipment and good sanitary facilities, the dread has been removed from childhood illnesses. Except in a few cases, children are restored to health and vigour after a week or two at home.

Another aspect of domestic life that has seen great change is childbirth. Many mothers still bear their babies at home, but an increasing number choose to give birth in a hospital environment. During our childhood there was little or no choice. A few private nursing homes were beginning to offer an alternative, but the fees were unaffordable for most families and besides, women had always had their babies at home and mothers saw no reason to change that system. A local midwife or the district nurse presided over the affair; their skill and knowledge in having brought hundreds of babies into the world gave confidence to the confined mother. There were surprisingly few fatalities; I personally never knew of anyone who lost a baby, or a mother who died during childbirth. Women remained in bed for about ten days after the birth, a welcome treat for mothers of large families, though they probably fretted to be up and about again, taking care of their children and attending to household tasks.

Often Grandma, an aunt or a neighbour, or sometimes even Father took care of the rest of the family until Mother was able to resume her duties, and a strange household it seemed, without her to preside over meals and baths and so on. The children visited her and the new baby in the bedroom, wondering and perhaps asking, where the new arrival had come from and why Mother had to stay in bed. We had not then reached the freedom of information era in which our own and subsequent children have grown up, taking for granted their early awareness of how reproduction takes place.

Some families were barely touched by the harsh economics of the twenties and thirties, while others suffered terribly, surviving on the dole or by whatever means possible. For the majority however, there were good and bad times; food, clothing and money were adequate but pennies were carefully counted; clothing was handed down the family or donated to other families who were in more desperate straits. Everyone worked hard for very moderate wages that covered the necessities of life but allowed for few luxuries. We yearned for expensive clothes and toys but never asked for them, knowing them to be unattainable. Simple things gave us great pleasure and contentment and we never perceived ourselves as being deprived. In fact, it was often pointed out to us that we were very fortunate compared with many families we either knew or heard of.

* * * * *

A KNOCK AT THE DOOR

Horse-drawn carts and vans delivered milk, bread, vegetables and coal to our doors on a daily or weekly basis and were a familiar sight as they made their rounds, the size and hauling capacity of the horses matched to the loads they were required to pull. Most carts required only one horse, but two were often harnessed to the heavy, flat coal carts with their hundred-weight sacks of coal. The big horses walked slowly when they set out with a full load, but as the load gradually lightened and the cart emptied, the horses picked up speed, their task a little easier until they once again left their yard with a further cargo of full sacks. The men who delivered the coal wore a leather garment that covered their back and shoulders for protection as they humped full sacks from the cart to the customer's storage area, known as the *coalplace*. With a loud rattle and clatter the coal was tipped out of the sacks from shoulder height, large lumps breaking and small pieces scattering in all directions.

Although bottled milk had begun to make an appearance, many families still bought their milk from old-fashioned milkmen who delivered it in large cans, often twice each day, after the morning and evening milking. We had two milkmen call on us: the morning milkman conveyed the heavy cans on the handlebars of his bicycle, which I don't think he rode until the cans were partly emptied; he pushed his bike along from house to house, propping it against the front gate or fence. At the door, our jugs were filled from pint, half pint and gill (quarter pint) measures that hung by long hooks from a rack inside the can. Straight from the cow, raw and unpasteurised, the rich milk acquired a deep layer of cream on top after standing in the jug for a short period of time.

Early in the evening an older man delivered milk to us. He rode in a little pony-drawn milk float, a small, two-wheeled vehicle with a rear access step; it was just large enough to hold the milkman and two cans of milk. The cans, opened at each house, probably absorbed a few particles of dust, a process that would be considered most unhygienic today, but we never gave it a thought. The milkmen were our friends, to be chatted with as they filled our jugs, asking after our families and imparting their own news. The days of a brief rattling of bottles on a doorstep and a milkman who only knocked on the door once each week to collect payment were still a few years into the future for many of us.

Once, when I was very ill and confined to a bedroom overlooking the back door, I used to listen for the milkman's cheery voice and the rattle of his can every morning; when I was well enough to get out of bed he called up to me and I leaned out of the window to talk to him. Best of all, on my birthday, when I was still isolated, he brought me a present of a small china doll, packed in a shoe box with a wardrobe of clothes sewn and knitted by his wife and daughter. Never did a gift delight me more.

In addition to regular tradesmen, there were other, occasional callers who came knocking at our doors, adding colour and interest to many an ordinary day. To recall them is to remember a way of life that is now as passé as the horse-drawn vehicle itself.

Occasionally during the summer months, the hurdy-gurdy man made an appearance. We may have been playing in the house, or outside, when from the street came the tinkling sound of the hurdy-gurdy. We ran out to watch and listen: the box-like barrel organ was mounted on two wheels with legs at the front to stabilise it when the owner stopped to give a performance. It was operated by a handle that was cranked round and round, scraping strings inside to produce the music.

We never questioned where the hurdy-gurdy man came from, where he lived, slept or ate, but he surely must have lived an entirely different life style from ours, so alien did he seem to us. He wore a bright red neckerchief tucked into his dark jacket and a brimmed hat pulled low over his forehead. He rarely spoke, but stood cranking the handle until the entire repertoire of tunes had been played, then went from house to house collecting pennies in his hat. Sometimes he had a tiny monkey with a collar round its neck to which was attached a chain that fastened to the top of the organ. He watched us with beady little eyes, occasionally jumping on his master's shoulder and making chattering noises.

The music brought most of the neighbourhood children into the street and when the performance was over and the hurdy-gurdy man lifted the shaft-like handles to wheel his instrument along to the next stopping place, we sometimes followed to listen to the music all over again. A tune that was a favourite was *Lily Of Laguna;* whenever I hear that tune, I'm immediately carried back to those childhood summer days.

The hurdy-gurdy man belonged to lazy summer days, with mothers leaning over front gates to listen. It was a pleasure that had survived from earlier generations and was soon to join the muffin man, the lamplighter and horse-drawn carriages as part of a nostalgic past. We were among the last children to enjoy street barrel organs.

In the early thirties when unemployment was rife and thousands of men were on the dole, life was exceptionally hard for those who had fought and had been wounded in The Great War and were physically unfit for the few jobs that were available. Some lived a bare existence, selling small items from door to door to help eke out a living. Several times I recall such men knocking at our door with trays of shoelaces, matches and other small items, some with an arm missing, blind in one eye or perhaps swinging along on crutches with a trouser leg pinned up over a stump. They were thin and haggard and must often have wondered whether all those months, even years in the trenches had been worth the loss of a limb or an eye, or worse, the loss of self-respect, if all that life could offer them afterwards was selling shoelaces. Life during those depression years was difficult for many; being poor was so normal that people didn't realise they were poor, only that others were rich, or comparatively so. But for men who had given their youth and health to fight for a better world it must have seemed doubly ironic, to say the least. My mother always bought something from them; her own father had fought in France and had been fortunate enough to survive without permanent injury. But for the Grace of God, she always declared, he might have been similarly maimed.

In stark contrast was the turbaned Indian who called on us, bringing an exotic, eastern aura. Suave and smiling, coffee-skinned and persuasive, he opened up on our doorstep a miniature bazaar from his bulging suitcase. The explosion of colour was dazzling.

"Nice Indian silks. Make your little girls nice dresses."

Everything to tempt the housewife was whisked out and draped over his arm: gaudy silk scarves for the ladies and plain white silk ones for men to wear with their best suits on Saturday night; lengths of fabric; table cloths and sideboard runners with eastern scenes woven, tapestry-like, into the material; and even underwear, flimsy and daring. The items were displayed like a rainbow, more and more being produced in an attempt to effect a sale. But such things were luxuries and even the offer to put an item aside until the money could be saved did not persuade our mother to buy. How she must have longed to indulge in something pretty and impractical, something for herself that wasn't utilitarian. My sisters and I longed for dresses made from the pretty material, but they were not for our life style and in any case, we already had Sunday dresses. The Indian salesman would be on the market on Friday if we changed our mind, displaying his wares on a stall, pretty scarves and other items fluttering gently in the breeze as they hung from a rack to tempt people who came from the surrounding area to shop.

Totally different from the Indian was the friendly and business-like lady who called regularly, also with a suitcase of goods, but of the type families like ours had to buy. When her case was opened it revealed sensible underwear for both children and women, items such as woollen vests and buttoned bodices, fleecy bloomers, long socks and woollen stockings, cardigans, skirts, warm gloves and scarves for winter. There were other items too: hankies, lavender bags for scenting drawers or giving as gifts; sewing necessities such as needles, pins, thread, tape, elastic and embroidery silks; in fact almost anything that was essential for home sewing and dressmaking. Our mother often made purchases from the lady and sometimes ordered things to be brought on her next visit. She had a system, to trusted customers, of allowing them to make weekly payments, which she called to collect.

Although the items were dull compared to the Indian's inventory, we loved to watch as the friendly saleslady took them from her case, one by one. The scent of new materials and the wintry smell of wool made us eager to have the new garments. It was like having a shop brought to our door and we crowded round in order not to miss anything. The visits had a social aspect too: the lady came to know her *clientele* and chatted with them, asking after the family as she displayed her wares.

There seemed so much more time then: no one had today's mania for rushing through the day, nor were there the pressures inherent in today's more materialistic society; there was always time to chat with a visitor at the door. Socially, people went out very little, so every opportunity to exchange ideas and news was a bright spot in the day.

From a nearby gypsy encampment, the women sometimes came knocking at our doors to sell clothes pins they made as they sat around their open fires or travelled along in their caravans. They carried them in flat, woven baskets that they also made themselves. Small children often accompanied the women, babies being carried papoose-wise in a fringed shawl.

We hung close to our mother when gypsies came to the door, giving them no opportunity to kidnap us in the manner we'd heard about, although as our mother pointed out, who would want to run off with us? Gypsies had enough children of their own.

Gypsy women were noted for their ability to foretell the future, though many people scoffed at such an idea and refused to take the predictions seriously. The gypsy usually made her pitch by divulging one tantalising, prophetic item of information, then offer to tell more if the householder "crossed her palm with silver". On occasions the predictions were accurate: my mother was once told, when I was very young, how many children she would have. Several years into the then future, that number turned out to be exact. The same gypsy forecast that some of those children would one day "cross the sea to live". In an era when few people of any class went abroad, even for holidays, it sounded implausible to say the least; during the following decade, thousands went overseas for very different reasons, many of them never to return. But today, three members of my family, including myself, live in Canada. Coincidence? Some would say so. On two occasions many years after that prediction, my husband and I were on the receiving end of gypsy predictions that eventually proved accurate. Perhaps they do have psychic powers.

Gypsies were colourful people, adding spice and a little excitement to our lives from time to time. The visits at our doors often ended with a request for old clothes, rags, bottles or anything else we wished to be rid of.

We usually saved that sort of thing for the rag and bone man who drove around the town with a horse and cart collecting anything that could be salvaged and re-sold. We saved rags in old potato sacks, but received very little for them in return. "Any old rags, bottles or bones?" heralded his approach, a signal to sort out whatever items we'd been saving for him. His cart, piled with sacks, bottles and jars, old metal bed ends, metal piping and other junk, rattled along the street, the weary-looking pony halting every few houses to allow its master to call out his cry and collect scrap items that householders wished to give away or sell for a few pennies.

A few other, perhaps less colourful callers came knocking at our doors occasionally. One was the man who sharpened knives and scissors; his foot-operated sharpening machine was parked by the roadside as he went from door to door collecting items to be sharpened. We heard the whirring sound as he honed them on the big wheel. We sometimes gave him scissors to sharpen, but our knives were sharpened either on the bone-handled steel belonging to the carving set or for a fast sharpening of a kitchen knife a few swishes back and forth either on the doorstep or on a small sharpening stone kept in a kitchen drawer.

Every few weeks a large horse-drawn van, later replaced by a motorised one, stopped out in the street, attracting the attention of neighbourhood women. The sides of the van were open, displaying a variety of kitchen ware. Saucepans and frying pans, brooms, mops and brushes, baskets, table ware as well as cooking and cleaning equipment were hung from racks or stacked in piles inside the van to tempt prospective buyers. We gathered round to admire the shiny pots and pans and listen to the sales pitch as the vendor pointed out his newest lines of merchandise and expounded on their durability and efficiency.

Occasionally our mother bought a much-needed item; a brush perhaps, or a saucepan, but consistent with the manner in which small incidents lodge in one's memory, I most clearly recall her buying pot menders. They were small, metal discs used in that era to repair holes in enamel or metal pots, bowls and dishes. The pot menders consisted of two discs with small, centre holes, a washer and a nut and bolt. One disc was placed over the hole on the outside of the vessel, the other on the inside, with a washer between them, then the bolt passed through the centre and fastened tightly with the nut, making the pot watertight again, at least for a while longer. Many of our saucepans and baking dishes were made of enamel and constant use on very hot coal ranges caused them to wear very quickly.

By far the most fascinating of all our callers were the tramps. In the early thirties they were numerous almost everywhere, a familiar sight along country roads. Some of them took to the life by choice and enjoyed being kings of the road, but many had no home, no job and often no family and the only way they could survive was by tramping the roads and begging for food or working a day or so here and there to earn enough to purchase the few necessities they needed.

Quite often they appeared at our doors early in the morning to request a billy can of boiling water to make tea after spending a night in the open. They always asked if there was a crust of bread to spare and most people gave them that, spread with lard, jam, or dripping from roasted meat. Everything they owned was carried on their person and some of the tramps presented an odd, rag-tag appearance. Clothing was whatever they may have retained from a former life style or had perhaps been donated to them along the way. Jackets and trousers were crumpled or torn and sometimes the men wore layers of jackets or coats, dependent upon the weather. Boots were their biggest problem; the endless walking wore them out quickly and I recall seeing tramps with toes sticking out of boots. A bundle of clothing and personal items tied in a red and white handkerchief and carried over the shoulder on a stick like Dick Whittington was a regular sight. Hung about their person were such necessary items as a billy can, a pocket knife, a tin mug and plate, knife and fork of cheap metal and a few other items deemed necessary for a nomadic way of life. Hats were varied: caps, soft tweed hats, bowlers, trilbies, in fact any available head gear that would give protection from sun and rain and serve as a pillow when its wearer laid himself down to sleep on the grass that was his bed at night.

At that time, the Whittlesey workhouse was still in use, though rarely for families, as in Dickensian days. A few transient or homeless people lodged here on a temporary basis, but mostly it was the tramps who used the workhouse as an overnight dormitory when they passed through the town. We lived close enough that we could see the buildings from our back yard and hear the bell that clanged to announce meal times or to indicate gate-opening time.

Every evening at six o'clock, the big iron gates swung open to admit tramps and other transients who wished to spend the night in the workhouse. It cost them, I recall being told, one penny for a bed and an additional penny or two for breakfast the following morning. If they were penniless they earned their night's lodging by doing chores.

Sometimes my sister and myself, along with neighbouring friends, used to walk as far as the workhouse after tea on summer evenings and wait to watch tramps being admitted. In retrospect, I don't know why we were so fascinated. We were accustomed to seeing them call at our homes, we saw them sitting by the roadside eating their hunks of bread and drinking tea from tin mugs or billy cans, yet we were still drawn to watch those raggedly-dressed itinerants gather *en masse*, patiently waiting on the grass verges by the side of the road, their bundles beside them, until the moment the bell would announce the opening of the workhouse gates.

We kept our distance though. We knew that most tramps were harmless, yet they still represented the "strange man syndrome" and we were suitably wary of them.

Promptly at six o'clock, the bell in the little tower atop the workhouse signalled the hour and the gates were opened from the inside by an official. The tramps rose wearily to their feet and shuffled across the road to enter the compound, the gates being closed again with a loud clang once the men were inside. Then we went home. *Watching the tramps go into the workhouse* was a fascinating pastime; I recall observing their clothing, bundles, funny hats - sometimes more than one at a time - and other accoutrements with great interest. What *they* thought of a group of curious young children staring at them can only be speculated upon.

That particular workhouse, in Victorian days the dreaded, last resort home of impoverished, despairing families, was demolished just prior to the second world war, its function obsolete in a world that was edging towards a welfare state. Before demolition began, the contents of the workhouse were auctioned off; my husband recalls attending the auction with a friend one day, when one of the lots that came under the auctioneer's hammer was a number of coffins. He doesn't remember who bought them.

After the war a large secondary school, now a community college, was built on the site and named after the town's great hero, Sir Harry Smith. For years after the school was built I found it difficult to pass the building without recalling the impressive old yellow-brick workhouse that stood there during my childhood. Even now, I can picture a group of tramps waiting to be admitted on a summer evening, while a huddle of young children, just a little bit scared, watch from a safe distance.

* * * * *

BESIDE THE SEASIDE

An event many children looked forward to each summer was the Sunday School outing, which took place towards the end of July. We almost always went to Hunstanton, our nearest seaside resort, though there were occasional deviations when a different place, perhaps Skegness, further along the coast, in Lincolnshire, was chosen instead. For the majority of children it was their only opportunity to see the sea during the entire summer and the anticipation of the outing during the preceding weeks was almost as exciting as the day itself.

The outing was always held on a Thursday, it being early closing day for local shops. They closed at one o'clock and staff were then free to enjoy their half day's holiday and participate in various leisure activities, if they wished. Sunday School teachers who worked in local businesses usually took a whole day off for the annual outing, though they may have had to forfeit wages or make up time later for the additional half day.

Once the date was announced, we children began to speculate on matters important to us. Which hotel would we go to this year for the traditional tea? Would it be a hot day? (It usually wasn't!). What would be the colour of the ribbon bows we'd wear to identify us as *bona fide* members of the Sunday School? I'm not sure why we considered the last item to be of such significance, but I recall stopping on my way to school each day to look at the big, flat rolls of narrow braid displayed in a window of the saddler's shop in High Street to guess which colour we might wear. The braid was sold to decorate the manes and tails of farm horses when they were dressed for show purposes and came in colours of red, blue, green and yellow. The braid was also purchased for other purposes, one of them being to make the little bows we wore for identification on our annual outing, each Sunday School having a different colour. I never did discover who cut and folded all those yards of braid and sewed them to tiny, brass safety pins. I remember saving them each year until I had one in each colour.

When the day of the outing finally arrived, we were up early to assemble in the church hall at six-thirty to be counted and have the all-important bow pinned on our coats. The hall seemed bare and alien at that hour on a weekday morning; we usually saw it on Sunday afternoons, set out with circles of chairs for Sunday School classes. We congregated from all parts of the town, some carrying pails and spades ready for digging on the beach, while others may have left those items with their parents. Having all been accounted for, we straggled along to the market place with our teachers, there to join up with the children from St. Mary's church. We belonged to St. Andrew's. The chapels and non-conformist churches held their outing on a different Thursday, often the week before ours. Once the two lots of children were lined up, we marched, not very smartly, to the railway station, shivering a little in the chill morning air. Parents, relatives and friends were on their way too, laden with spades and pails, towels and extra clothing, babies and toddlers and bags or cases containing sandwiches for our lunches. During my earlier childhood, I recall the town band heading our little parade, giving us a rousing send-off to the day. I'm not sure that residents of the houses we passed would have been enthusiastic at being awakened by a band at that hour of the morning, though it's true that many of them would have been up and about to begin their working day.

After arriving at the station we sorted ourselves out into families, anxiously seeking mothers, brothers and sisters who had either followed the parade or waited at the station. Very few fathers went along, they could rarely take time from the more important task of earning a living.

The station platform was crowded, but the special train soon arrived and we scrambled for seats, pleased to get in and settle down for the journey. Glad too, to rest after such an early start; the march to the station and probably a lack of sleep the previous night, due to excitement and anticipation, had drained much of our energy. Bags, clothing and sandwiches were stowed away in overhead racks, doors locked and dire warnings issued by parents not to touch the emergency bell cord. How we longed to pull that cord to find out if it really did stop the train! But the penalty for misuse was five pounds, an enormous sum of money at that time, more than many of our fathers earned in a week.

When I was older, I was travelling home from school one day on the train along that same line when someone *did* pull the emergency cord, bringing the train to a halt a few miles outside the town. The guard left his van at the rear of the train and walked along the tracks, suspecting, I'm certain, the grammar school boys. None of them was ever proved guilty and the train resumed its journey after a brief delay.

The beginning of our journey to the seaside was over familiar ground and we recognised local landmarks, but after a few minutes and a few miles had passed we spent more time looking out of the windows at new and different sights. Even the animals in the fields appeared different and we played games to pass the time, perhaps spotting white horses or black pigs. We looked for our grandparents' house, knowing they'd be watching the train, Grandfather through his binoculars. Past the town of March with its extensive railway yards and sidings, we soon came to the Wisbech area, where we marvelled at plum and apple orchards, their thousands of trees standing in lines as straight and orderly as a regiment of soldiers. After a stop at King's Lynn came the always baffling experience of the train appearing to reverse, starting to take us back home again, until it was explained that the train was branching off to another line and sure enough, a few minutes later, looking out of the window, it was possible to see the entire length of the train as it rounded a curve in the track.

The really exciting stretch of the journey began after King's Lynn. We soon approached the Sandringham area, where King George and Queen Mary owned a large country house surrounded by acres of estates and woods, farms and gardens. The soil along the embankment beside the track in that region was very sandy and pitted with rabbit burrows; we peered from the windows hoping for a glimpse of a rabbit, though we rarely saw one. Then came Wolferton, the King's station, where he used to alight from his train to be driven to Sandringham. The station, small and prettily-situated in densely-treed woods, was spic and span with bright paint and neat flower beds. Large rhododendron shrubs bloomed profusely beside the railway track and in the woods beyond; the landscape was very different from the flat farmland we'd left less than an hour earlier.

Our destination drew nearer: Dersingham, Snettisham, then Heacham, where we strained for a first glimpse of the sea that usually appeared as a narrow, greyish strip on the horizon, barely distinguishable from the sky.

But if the day was sunny, there would be that magical glint of sun on water, with perhaps a distant fishing boat or sail boat to complete the picture.

At that point we began to assemble our belongings, don our coats, blazers or cardigans and gather up our pails and spades, as we had almost reached our destination. Within a few minutes the train came to a halt at Hunstanton station, a pleasure alas, that no future generations of children will ever experience: British Rail, in its doubtful wisdom, saw fit to demolish that once much-used terminus and time-honoured entrance to our nearest coastal resort. Now, cars choke the roads every weekend and holiday season; one wonders whether drivers and their passengers, as they sit and fume at traffic jams and the slowness of their journey, would not prefer to travel by train in comfort and relaxation, as we did so many years ago.

We've finally arrived! Such an exodus and clanking of metal pails and excited running back and forth and the smell of the sea and fish and the ozone-y air. Will the tide be in? We hope not, for that means we won't be able to go on the beach right away, but will have to stay up on the promenade until the water has receded far enough to allow family groups to settle on the sands. We make our way from the station and ... look ... the tide is out! We hurry past the stalls selling shrimps, cockles and whelks, past the kiosks on the promenade festooned with spades, beach balls, kites, bathing suits and big straw hats and run down the steps to the beach. The sand is fine and dry because the high tide didn't reach that far; it oozes through our toes when we take our shoes off. But beyond those few yards of dry sand there is an enormous expanse of damp, smooth, firm sand, pock-marked with raised squiggles where tiny sand crabs have emerged and disappeared again. Our bare feet make squelchy sounds and leave imprints on the virgin, sea-washed beach as we cover the long distance to the water to splash in the waves before returning to our family's staked-out portion of beach to begin the serious business of digging moats and building sand castles. On the way back from the water we search for crabs and starfish, seaweed and other tiny creatures in the small pools formed between rocks by the out-going tide.

We have several hours before the tide turns and waves wash our sand castles away to become part of the sea bed once again. We run back and forth to the water all day, boys with their shorts rolled high on their thighs, girls with dresses tucked into bloomers. The water may be too cold to bathe, but many of us do not, in any case, own bathing suits. Mothers and other adults take off their shoes and stockings and tuck up their clothing to paddle ceremoniously in the shallow water at the edge of the waves, easing corns and bunions on their white feet, younger children holding tightly to their hands as they are introduced, often unwillingly, to their first, sometimes frightening experience of such a vast expanse of water. Men wear straw boaters or handkerchiefs knotted at the four corners to protects their heads from sun or wind and ladies wear straw hats with brims, or close-fitting cloches.

The men who hire out deck chairs ply their business along the beach and those who can afford to, also hire a canvas screen to protect them from the wind, forming a cosy, sunny shelter where they can sit and bask in the trapped sun, if sun there be. Others settle near breakwaters, hoping for protection against the wind from those long, wooden barriers that reach right out into the water. Our coast is not a mild and gentle one, except on rare occasions and children often need to wear warm cardigans or coats as they dig in the sand, their hair and clothing whipped by breezes that blow across the bay of The Wash from the North Sea.

Having made such an early start to the day we soon begin to feel hungry and pester our mothers to bring out the sandwiches that we eat with gusto and sandy fingers. Never did fish paste sandwiches or tomatoes with bread and butter taste as good as on that windy, sunny beach. We are ravenous and there are never enough sandwiches to satisfy our appetites. Our mothers have tried to position themselves on the beach so that they are conveniently near the café at the end of the pier where tea is sold in jugs. They carry the steaming beverage back to the beach on a tray with provided cups. We manage to get a drink of tea after the adults have had theirs, then we walk back to the café with them to return the jugs and cups and reclaim the deposit. We have carefully-hoarded pennies in our pockets with which we buy Lyon's ice cream, sold in firm, cylindrical slices with cardboard wrappers that we peel off before inserting the ice cream into cornets. They are delicious, to be licked slowly as we return to the beach. The crowds have thinned out a little, some families having decided to go into the town for fish and chips or other such delights at one of the many restaurants.

Another penny must be spent on a donkey ride, without which a visit to the seaside is incomplete. We each choose a donkey and perch uncomfortably on its bony back as a boy leads us from one breakwater to the next and back again. Not a very long ride for the money, our mothers complain. There may be a Punch and Judy show on the beach and if so, a large crowd of children soon gathers to watch the age-old drama being played out, all of us shouting at the puppets and holding our breath, laughing and clapping, wanting it to continue, even after the story has been told and the show ended.

During the afternoon we take a walk along the cliff tops to Old Hunstanton, then descend a long flight of steps to the beach where we clamber among slippery rocks while the adults sit in the shelter of the tall cliffs to rest. We continue along the beach to the pier, then go up to the promenade and stroll along to watch paddle boats on the boating lake or investigate the amusement park. We make sure we are back at The Green by four o'clock, the hour we'll be summoned to assemble for tea at a nearby hotel. Our Sunday School superintendent rings a bell that sounds like a town crier's bell, bringing us rushing from the sands or promenade to the wide, high, grassy area overlooking the beach; there we are shepherded into lines by our teachers, who check our identification bows. Then we are marched to a hotel room where a tea has been set out for us. Not a very remarkable meal seen in retrospect, but sandwiches, plain bread and butter, fruit cake and plain cake and lemonade or tea are a feast when we had begun the day at six-thirty and had eaten our lunches several hours earlier. With strict instructions to look after younger brothers and sisters and make sure they have enough to eat, we demolish the plates of food and exchange the day's experiences with friends.

With appetites more or less sated, we rejoin our families who have meanwhile partaken of their own meal; then depending on tide and weather, we decide how to spend the remaining, precious hours of the day, now disappearing all too quickly. If the tide is high, we watch from the promenade as waves hit the sea wall and splash spray into our faces. Deck chair men collect their chairs and stack them in piles on the promenade ready for tomorrow's visitors.

If the tide is out, we play on the beach again and go down to the water for a final paddle, running back and forth in the ripply waves that gradually advance towards the families still on the beach. Pails of water are carried back to rinse our feet and we vainly attempt to dry them and put on socks and shoes without getting sand inside. Sand will inevitably be there the next day, a gritty but happy reminder of yesterday's pleasure. Shoes on and baggage collected, we walk out to the end of the pier to watch huge waves bash against the iron girders; we feel very vulnerable as we look down at the deep, surging water below.

Our final commission of the day is to buy small gifts to take home. Sticks of pink, peppermint rock for ourselves and an extra one for Dad; if Grandma hadn't been with us on the outing, we buy something for her, usually a small, china ornament that says *A Present From Hunstanton*, to add to her collection displayed in a glass-fronted china cabinet in her bedroom. For Grandpa, shrimps or a bloater or perhaps a small novelty and also a jar of whelks for Dad.

It's finally time to leave and we wend our way back to the station, damp towels and clothing filling the bags, our pails heavy with seaweed and shells and becoming a burden to carry in arms that feel increasingly tired as the long, exciting day draws to a close; we drag our feet in exhaustion. Young children are whiny and sleepy and have to be coaxed along, but the train is waiting and we board it with relief. Sticks of rock are unwrapped and as we suck on their minty sweetness we speculate, as we do every year, on how the word *Hunstanton*, is made to permeate the entire length and still be readable. Last minute arrivals rush on to the platform and search for seats; we lean out of the windows as final preparations are made for the train's departure. The guard blows his whistle, waves his green flag and we are off, our long-anticipated day almost over. Crowding at the windows for a last glimpse of the sea, we wave Good-bye, possibly until next year, unless we have the good fortune to make a further trip before the end of the summer, though for many of us, that's an improbability.

The train ride home is quieter than the exciting morning journey and gradually we begin to fall asleep, one by one, or we stare out of the window, not speaking, our thoughts still on the day's events.

When the train pulls into our own station there are several fathers waiting on the platform to help with baggage and sleepy children and to hear about our day. The crowd of mothers, fathers and children winds along Station Road, thinning gradually as families turn off into streets leading home. Having reached home, we fall into bed and are asleep almost immediately, scarcely remembering the next morning how we got there.

Tomorrow we'll live it all again, empty the sand from our shoes, hang up the bunches of seaweed and look at them every day to tell the weather; open seaweed pods indicate a fine day, closed up tightly means it will rain. The shells we collected will be kept as souvenirs, along with our horse-braid bow and the last of the peppermint rock will be eaten.

It was all over for another year!

In recent years I have travelled many thousands of miles by land, sea and air and have vacationed in some of the world's most spectacular scenery, but no journey or holiday has ever given me more pleasure, nor is remembered more vividly than that short trip across the fens to spend a day at Hunstanton each summer. Even now, when I visit the resort and see the hundreds of cars in the streets and parking lots, the well-appointed holiday caravans and people with their pockets full of money to spend, I recall the poignancy of the simple pleasures we so looked forward to and enjoyed long ago, when the world was a far less complicated place than it is today.

The Green is still there and to me it echoes with the voices of children assembling for a Sunday School tea; it's still pleasant to walk along the cliff tops or between rocks on the beach; children still lick ice creams and play in the waves and build sand castles; fishing boats still bob up and down out in The Wash; and everywhere, I see children in old-fashioned clothes, children belonging to an age when happiness was a single day at the seaside with a few pennies to spend.

* * * * *

HORSE POWER

Horses on the streets were as familiar during our childhood as motorised vehicles are to modern children. They pulled delivery carts, farm wagons, gypsy caravans, funeral coaches and in fact provided a means of transportation that in most sectors has now been totally replaced by motor power. Public transport was of course motorised by the 1920's and 30's, but horses were still widely used for commercial purposes both in cities and in the country.

Steaming horse buns, dropped casually along streets, have been replaced by the pervading smell of petrol and diesel fuel. Horse excreta could at least be scooped up and used as manure and did permanent harm to no one; the fumes from petrol and oil on the other hand, are a contributing factor to the conglomeration of chemicals from industry and transport that spew into the atmosphere, assailing our nostrils and in the name of progress polluting the air that was once sullied mainly by nature's smells.

There were many cars on the roads when we were children, but in small towns like ours, few families owned a car solely for pleasure. It was affluent families, professional people such as doctors, and a minority of the business community who were able to afford such a luxury; and perhaps a few young, mostly single people, exhilarated by the freedom of such a novel mode of travel and eager to cut a dash in open cars with running boards and dickey seats, their hair streaming in the wind.

All summer, red farm wagons pulled by magnificent Shires, Percherons, Clydesdales and other working horses rumbled past our house loaded with hay, peas, grain, sugar beet, potatoes and other crops according to season. Often a string of wagons came, a procession of might and colour, the great feet of the heavy horses pounding the road surface, their harness and brass jingling as they hauled the huge loads along.

I remember the hay wagons with a particular nostalgia as they passed several times each day on their journeys to and from the hayfields along the Wash road, their loads so high and broad they appeared top-heavy. Often we were playing in the street as they approached and when they reached us, we used to run behind them, pulling out handfuls of hay. The men leading the horses shouted at us, but the next time they passed we did the same thing again.

With their large, wooden wheels and their design almost unchanged for generations, the farm wagons evoked a primeval feeling, like being part of an historical pageant as it happened, rather than enacting it years later. In retrospect, we were subjects of Constable-like paintings come to life as we witnessed the final stages of horse-drawn transportation. Although we didn't realise it at the time, we were participants in a segment of history that would later be regarded as the end of an era.

On farms and smallholdings horses pulled ploughs and other implements across the black, fertile fen fields, the men who worked them and cared for them not realising that within a comparatively short period of time almost all the horses would be replaced by tractors. Some farmers looked forward to mechanisation while others lamented the passing of horses from the position they had held in farming history for hundreds of years.

The horsekeeper on a farm was an employee of importance: not only did he care for the horses and prepare them for their daily work in the fields, he also groomed them for the agricultural shows that were - and still are - held all over the country. The cream of the Percherons, Suffolks, Shires and other breeds were transported to most of the major shows to compete against others of their ilk. Groomed as carefully and meticulously as beauty queen contestants, their manes were braided and tied with ribbon, their rippling, muscular bodies adorned with burnished leather and gleaming brasses before being led into the show ring. The showing of heavy horses, either alone or in teams with newly-painted wagons, are still the highlight of agricultural shows, admired not only by farmers and farm workers, but by everyone who is at heart a countryman or woman or who appreciates such might and magnificence. Though they no longer serve their masters as horse power of the original kind, a number of heavy horses are still kept for show purposes and it is with a sense of nostalgia that older men now go to watch and admire them, remembering the days when they walked miles up and down the long fields, exposed to all weathers, behind a Captain or Prince or Bess.

Everyone, in city and country alike, was familiar with horses in the streets: they delivered our bread, milk, vegetables, coal and other commodities and were mostly good-natured beasts that knew their daily routes as well as did their masters. We have all seen the horse that knew exactly how many houses to pass before halting to allow the driver to re-load his basket with bread or collect a new crate of milk bottles. Then with a word or whistle, the horse ambled off to its next stop, where it waited again.

Most of the delivery horses were sleek, well-groomed animals and obviously well cared for, but there were an unfortunate few that were old and tired and might have been far happier grazing in a retirement paddock, away from the daily round.

In country towns like ours, many of the roads had grass verges on one or both sides and sometimes a horse decided to do a little grazing while its master was about his business, often causing the cart to twist across the road, blocking other traffic. A few choice words from the driver when he returned usually put the situation to rights and reminded the horse of its duties.

Nosebags always fascinated me: I thought it intriguing that a horse could eat its dinner from a bag slung over its head and I recall that one day we tried it ourselves with paper bags and broken up biscuits or something similar in the bottom, pretending they were oats. Tossing the bag up to get the food into my mouth I almost choked myself and that was the end of playing at being a horse! Another factor I found most interesting was that on hot, summer days, horses that were exposed to heat for long periods of time sometimes wore straw hats, with their ears sticking out through holes. According to the whim of the owner or driver, some hats were even decorated with flowers. Very smart, I thought!

One day a most dramatic incident occurred: a horse died on the road outside the house next door to us. It was harnessed to a cart at the time, though I have no recall now of whose cart or of what type. It happened on a Saturday morning, so we were at home. There was a crash, then hearing the shouts of the driver we rushed to the front gate to see what the commotion was about. The poor horse lay quite still on the road, its legs stretched out stiffly. The shafts had been pulled down with it, tipping the cart to the front; the cart was empty at the time, so there was no load to spill.

When our mother realised the horse was dead, she hustled us back into the house, where we were allowed only to watch from the window, which was most frustrating as a thick hawthorn hedge hid some of the ongoing drama from our eyes. I cannot now recall, if I ever knew, whether the horse slipped and fell, collapsed from exhaustion or whether it suffered something akin to a heart attack. It lay there for half an hour or so, a source of great interest to passers-by, most of whom stopped to investigate the situation and offer condolences to the owner.

Soon a lorry appeared on the scene; the poor dead animal was winched on to it and taken away to the knacker's yard to be made into pet food and whatever else dead horses were then used for. We didn't know about that, but were more than likely under the impression it was being taken away to be given a decent burial.

George Johnson, who kept the popular and busy sweet shop in Market Street, also made delicious ice cream during the summer and most afternoons he drove around the town in a gaily-painted little cart drawn by a dark brown pony to sell cornets and wafers filled with custardy-tasting ice cream that always contained slivers of ice, cold and crunchy when one bit on them. The cart was painted green, yellow and white, had two large wheels and a canopy supported by a pole at each corner of the cart. Often on Friday evenings at the weekly market or when a fair was in town the cart was drawn to the market place by the pony, which was then led away and the cart, supported by a post at each corner, became a temporary stall that was kept busy selling ices to the passing crowds.

On summer afternoons though, the clopping of the pony's hooves and the tinkling of the bell that heralded its arrival sent us running to the front gate, either to buy a halfpenny cornet or at times to stand and gaze longingly as other children came away licking theirs. If we earned extra pennies during the summer we almost always saved them to buy ice cream.

I liked to watch Mr. Johnson make wafers: one of the wafer biscuits was placed in the bottom of the wafer-making mold, ice cream pressed deftly on top of it, the edges being smoothed off like a bricklayer smoothing mortar from around a brick. Another wafer biscuit was placed on top of the ice cream, then by releasing a spring the completed wafer popped out of the gadget. An adjustment could be made to alter the thickness of the wafer, a thin one for a penny, a thick one for two pence. I longed for a wafer when I was a child, they seemed so grown-up and sophisticated, but when I finally tried one I discovered they weren't as appealing as they appeared. The ice cream melted and dribbled down the edges, especially on hot days and it was a race against time to lick it fast enough to prevent the whole thing from disintegrating. I decided a penny cornet could be made to last much longer than a penny wafer.

An incident that occurred on one of those summer afternoons now seems highly amusing, but wasn't particularly so at the time. Hearing the tinkle of the ice cream man's bell, we asked our mother if we could have a cornet. It was obviously a day when she had no spare pennies and jokingly, she replied to the effect that we could have one if we could get it for nothing, then returned to her household duties. I was about seven years old at the time and without further ado, led my brother and two sisters out to the ice cream cart and asked for four halfpenny cornets. Mr. Johnson handed them to us, then asked for the two pennies, at which time I informed him that our mother had told us we could have them for nothing. Knowing she would not say such a thing, Mr. Johnson suggested I return for the money, but I was adamant about their being free. At that point, an aunt who lived a few houses away came out to buy ice cream and upon discovering what had transpired, paid for our ices. Imagine the expression of astonishment on our mother's face as the four of us walked into the house licking ices with great satisfaction. Our aunt followed to explain the situation. I have no recollection of what followed, but I'm sure my mother probably exclaimed, "What *will* that child think of next!" She must also have blamed herself just a little for not having given us an unqualified *No* when we asked for ice cream. I like to think I was both resourceful and naive; we could hardly have returned the ices, but I had interpreted my mother's jocular remark literally and genuinely believed we had her permission to obtain free ices. I'm sure there were a few laughs after that among the adults. Behind our backs, of course!

In stark contrast to the ice cream pony, was the tired-looking horse that belonged to the rag and bone man; it looked as though it too, had been a cast-off, along with the assortment of items on the flat, rattling cart that it pulled from house to house. As the cart, giving the appearance of a mobile junk yard, became heavier, the horse plodded along more and more slowly, no doubt longing for the day to end so that it could bed down for a well-earned rest before setting out again the next day to collect the flotsam of local households.

Another horse that paid a regular weekly visit to our neighbourhood was one we rarely saw: it came in the dead of night, pulling the night soil cart, the *honey cart*. We sometimes heard it, the horse's hooves clopping on the quiet road, the cart wheels grinding along, halting at each house, the voices drifting up to us in our bedrooms as they went about their obnoxious task of collecting pails of human waste, emptying them into the deep, trough-like cart then returning the pails to outside privies. Sometimes it became necessary to close the bedroom window until the horse and cart with its malodorous load had passed by.

Now that almost every household enjoys the benefits of a hygienic sanitation system it's unlikely that such arrangements exist anywhere in the country; the *honey cart* would seem primitive and unacceptable to modern families, though it was considered quite normal during our childhood. Not nice, but normal! The stinking pails must have been ideal breeding grounds for infection-carrying bacteria, no matter how well people tried to disinfect them and keep the outside toilets clean.

Looking back, one must admire the men who carried out that very necessary but odious task. The sound and smell of the fetid little procession in the middle of the night is one of the less pleasant memories of childhood. The horses too, must surely have envied their brothers and sisters who were fortunate enough to be employed in pulling milk carts, bread vans or almost any other type of commodity from house to house.

The gypsies are coming!

On hearing that cry, we rushed to the front gate or if we'd been playing in the street, ran back inside to watch from safety. I doubt the gypsies gave a passing thought to us, seeing us merely as a group of curious faces peering at them, but if you were a small child and gypsies were about to pass your house, you took no chances. Much as we feared them, we were nonetheless fascinated by them and watched their comings and goings with interest. A gypsy encampment was located not very far from where we lived and whenever those nomadic people arrived or departed, they passed along our street.

It was almost like watching a circus. Usually there was a string of a dozen or so caravans, brightly-painted and romantic in appearance with their rounded tops and an assortment of pails, cooking pots and other household items hanging from hooks underneath the vans or along the sides. The horses that drew the caravans were a motley collection of animals of various sizes and colours and in varying degrees of fitness. Gypsies were well-known as horse dealers and besides those pulling the caravans there were extra ones tied behind or being led by men and boys. Some of the horses gave the impression they were made from left-overs of other horses: there were patchy ones in blacks and browns; grey ones with white and black markings; rough-coated ponies that looked as though different colours had been appliquéed on to their backs and there were lean, dark brown ponies with flowing manes and a wild appearance.

It all caused a great deal of noise and excitement. The wheels of the caravans grinding long, the clip-clopping of the horses' hooves, jingling harness and the barking of dogs. There were always a number of dogs, often greyhounds, tied by long leashes to the caravans so that they ran alongside. Men and boys shouted as they urged the horses along and called to the dogs or to each other. Smaller boys ran up to us as we watched over the gate, made faces at us and sent us scurrying away, afraid of their swarthy looks and dark, flashing eyes.

The caravans interested me most and I never tired of watching them, trying to visualise the interiors but able only to obtain a tantalising glimpse inside as they passed by. I marvelled that an entire family lived in such a tiny space, slept there and stored their worldly possessions. I wished that just once I could step inside and see for myself how everything fitted in. The gypsy women sat in the doorways as they travelled along, babies in their arms, small children beside them, surveying the scene as the procession made its way along the streets. They wore their long, black, oily hair braided into coils over their ears, making them all look very much alike. Many of the little girls wore their hair in a similar fashion. Most dressed in long, dark skirts with shawls around their shoulders, younger women often carrying a baby in their shawls. Men wore dark clothing with a bright scarf around their necks beneath a collarless shirt. They soon settled into the camp, with outdoor fires burning, stews in cooking pots hanging over the fires, children and dogs racing about and horses grazing on the sparse grass.

When it became necessary to walk by the camp, we did so as

quickly as possible, eyeing the gypsies warily, afraid of the dark, piercing eyes that watched us and the dogs that set up a cacophony of barking as we hurried past.

The women were soon at our doors selling clothes pegs and school age children turned up in classrooms sporadically, grasping a few days of learning here and there, but never attending school regularly, to the despair of the education department truant officer.

There are still gypsies who follow the traditional, nomadic way of the ancient Romany tribes, but they travel now in motorised homes with modern conveniences, the old-fashioned, horse-drawn caravans having passed to a few romantics who spend holidays in them, travelling the back roads, trying to recapture the peace and serenity of an age that has gone forever.

In the days when everyone travelled by horse-drawn vehicle, which was before our time, country people travelled very little at all. Those who owned their own conveyance or needed it for their work, often had a pony and trap to trot around the countryside on visits and errands; farmers had their wagons or rode horseback and most other people used their own two feet, *shanks' pony*.

If a villager needed to go to the nearest town, he often travelled with the local carrier and when I was very young, that mode of travel was still used by some country folk who had no bus service convenient to their home. The carrier had been a country institution for generations, transporting both goods and people once or twice each week from outlying villages to a central market town. Early in the morning, almost always on market day, the carrier collected a variety of freight from residents along his route, either to deliver to the market or to an address along his route. Persons wishing to travel with him arrived at his departure point early, paid their penny or two and sat up front with the carrier. The journey was slow as crates of chickens, garden produce, parcels and other commissions were collected and delivered.

Arriving at the market town several miles distant, the carrier delivered his cargo to its assigned destinations, then put up his horse and cart for a few hours, usually at an inn or public house, where other carriers from surrounding villages and towns were arriving with their horses and carts.

By the middle of the afternoon, freight for the return journey was being delivered to the carrier and along with commissions he had carried out for customers, his cart soon began to fill up again. By late afternoon he was on his way, passengers beside him, often loaded with their own parcels and purchases. The horse jogged along, stopping at intervals for the carrier to deliver packages, crates and sacks. By the time he arrived home it was often late in the evening, the horse plodding tiredly, the passengers dozing.

During my childhood there were still carriers in our region of the country, plying their business by means of horse-drawn carts. Today, the occupation of carrier is extinct. Vast numbers of people have cars and carry their own shopping, lorries deliver heavy goods of all types from shops and businesses to points far and wide, and even remote villages are connected by bus services to towns and cities.

I'll send it with the carrier, or *We'll go into town with the carrier* are phrases no longer a part of country lore. They have become as obsolete as the horse-drawn carrier cart itself.

The modern funeral cortege is a sterile affair, submerged in the traffic that surrounds it; sleek, smoothly-purring cars follow an equally sleek hearse, often to a crematorium where, in the tranquillity of a pleasant chapel set amidst lawns and flowers, final religious rites are observed in an atmosphere far removed from the ostentation and laments of old-time funerals and wakes.

Death, with its accompanying grief, tragedy and loss is as devastating now as it ever was to bereaved families and friends, but to most other people a funeral is none of their concern.

When I was a child a local funeral assumed all the elements of a pageant. For several years my family lived a few hundred yards from the town cemetery and almost all funerals passed our house, so that I have a vivid recollection of many of those slow, stately processions, both humble and opulent, that carried the departed to their final resting place in style and with a modicum of pomp.

We usually knew when a funeral was to take place; in a small town such information is common knowledge. Along the funeral route blinds were lowered as a mark of respect, but it was also necessary to leave a few inches of peep space at the bottom to observe the procession as it passed! How many coaches would there be? How many wreaths? Who would be there? Our interest was part curiosity, part regret for the passing of the deceased, allied with compassion for the bereaved family, especially as we often knew them, sometimes well, sometimes only as casual acquaintances. We children were never allowed to stand outside and watch, that would have been considered brazen and disrespectful. Persons walking or cycling along the route as a funeral passed, stood in silence, men with cap in hand, all with heads bowed. If we were playing outdoors as a funeral approached, we were called indoors; I recall kneeling on a chair at the window to watch - beneath the blind - the passing drama.

Heading the procession was the undertaker, on foot and by tradition wearing a top hat and tail coat; behind him walked the clergyman who was to conduct the graveside service, his white surplice billowing out, prayer book in his hands. Then followed the glass-enclosed, horse-drawn hearse, travelling at a carefully-gauged pace in order to remain the correct distance behind the two men on foot. The horses that pulled the hearse were almost always black and occasionally wore black plumes as part of their funeral adornment. A few wreaths lay on the coffin, visible through the glass sides of the hearse. Alongside, walked the pallbearers, also dressed in black or dark suits. If the funeral was that of a prominent or affluent person, the pallbearers too, might wear top hats and formal dress. Funeral coaches followed the hearse, they also being drawn by black or dark brown horses. The faces of the mourners were visible through the coach windows, their faces white and strained against their black clothing. Everyone wore mourning then, it would have been unthinkable not to do so and some families who could ill afford the expense went into debt to comply with the now out-moded custom. The number of coaches was determined by the wealth, or lack of it, of the bereaved family, the size of the family and sometimes, regrettably, the impression a family wished to make on local residents. Sometimes there were only one or two coaches, the rest of the mourners following on foot.

The funeral coach was rather like a stage coach, with two seats inside, facing each other and a seat outside for the driver. The horses were always well-groomed, sleek animals and in compliance with the wishes of the deceased's family, either adorned with black ribbons or plumes, or left unadorned. The Victorian custom of lavish funeral decorations had by then almost disappeared. If the funeral were a large one, a flat cart sometimes followed the coaches, entirely covered with wreaths, to be laid on the grave after the interment.

It always seemed there ought to be slow music playing as the procession wended its way along, but the clopping of the horses' feet in the otherwise quiet street was almost as impressive. For some funerals a single church bell tolled as a mark of respect, adding an additional, solemn note.

There were individual funerals I recall as being a little out of the ordinary. A child's funeral was always sad and on those occasions, as a child myself, I was touched, wanting to cry. Children take it for granted that adults die, but the death of a contemporary was a startling reminder that it could happen to us too. In those days of epidemics and serious, infectious diseases, it happened more often than in present times and there were even occasions when the funeral was for a child we knew well. Coffins for children were always white, as they are today and the sight of a small, white coffin lying in the big, black hearse was a painful and tragic sight.

I remember seeing a baby's funeral at which there were no coaches at all, not even a hearse. My mother told me the family was very poor. The sad little procession of the baby's family walked by, two men carrying the tiny coffin, the few family members walking behind, not even in mourning clothes. The clergyman walked at the head, his dignity and bearing not in the least diminished by the poverty of the bereaved family.

Another funeral I clearly recall was that of a young man of eighteen who had worked at the same brickyard as my father. On his way to work one day he'd been killed by a train at a level crossing near the brickyard. A gruesome fact of the accident, one that stuck in my ever-receptive mind, was that his body had been carried for some distance along the track by the train. Almost all the yard's employees attended the funeral and I vividly remember the long column of men walking behind the coaches three or four abreast, their boots pounding on the tarmac; they resembled an army corps marching past. I watched with my mother, discreetly of course, and picked out my father among the mourners. To this day, like a photographic slide flashed before my eyes, I can see his young, pale face turning to glance briefly at his own house as he passed. It was a very sad occasion and a great shock to the men to have one of their number so suddenly and tragically killed.

Occasionally, by request of a deceased person's family, or perhaps to comply with the deceased's own request, a coffin was transported to the cemetery on a farm wagon. In such cases, the families were either farmers or smallholders, perpetuating a tradition dating back centuries, when a farm wagon may have been the only available vehicle. It seemed both primeval and impressive to watch the noble farm horses carry their master to his final resting place and one wonders whether they sensed the significance of the occasion.

Many children who lived in the town at that time probably witnessed very few funerals. To us they were a factor of everyday life as they passed our house. We did not perceive them as being morbid; they happened, we watched and waited until the horse-drawn procession had passed, then continued with our play. We saw them as we saw the passing of the hay carts, delivery vans and other vehicles, an accepted fact of our lives that would continue for ever. We never dreamed that before we were grown up a transportation revolution would have taken place and the stately funerals would become just another nostalgic memory.

A custom that used to be associated with horse-drawn vehicles was that of spreading straw on the road outside the house of a chronically ill person. It originated when many streets were cobbled and the noise of wooden wheels and clopping hooves on the cobbles was a day-long occurrence that no doubt reverberated through bedrooms that were often situated directly above streets. The thickly-spread straw deadened the noise to some degree and supposedly made the invalid's stay in bed a little more peaceful and an aid to recovery. I recall seeing straw on roads a few times during my early childhood and remember older people discussing it, but like the horse-drawn traffic that decreed the practice, it was by then on the point of becoming obsolete.

Today, the sound of cart wheels and clopping horses would seem almost idyllic and if recovery from illness depended upon silence, few patients would recover. Drugs and antibiotics have replaced the complete rest once considered an essential element in the treatment of illness and a few days in bed, rather than several weeks, usually cures most of us of our ills.

The horse-drawn vehicles that were in everyday use during my childhood are now, for the most part, restricted to parades, nostalgic events and ceremonial occasions. Farm wagons, drays, pony traps, four-in-hand teams and the like can be seen at agricultural shows and other horsey events, with public interest in them probably keener than when they plied our streets and country roads on their daily business. Royalty, Lord Mayors and other eminent personages travel on state occasions in carefully preserved, historic coaches while the rest of us admire them and maybe even feel slightly envious of such a romantic mode of travel.

Romance though, was far from the minds of travellers who had no choice when stage coaches, carrier carts, private carriages and horseback were the only available method of travelling around the country. Driving a coach, cart or pony and trap along a modern road may be nostalgic fun; driving or riding in them along the rough roads and rutted, muddy or frozen lanes of pre-mechanised days was often hazardous and almost certainly uncomfortable. Cars and buses may be noisy or crowded, but one arrives at one's destination warm and dry. Cars may become involved in accidents, but coaches and carts sometimes over-turned or may even have been held up by highwaymen, and horses often slipped on icy streets.

The good old days, when horses were the only available horse power were in many respects tranquil, but perhaps we tend to see them through rose-tinted glasses.

* * * * *

OUT SHOPPING

Remembering Whittlesey as it was when I was a child, I often think of the shops. One of my favourite outings was to stroll along Market Street on a Saturday afternoon or evening with my mother, brothers and sisters and perhaps my grandma, to buy or window-shop and to eavesdrop on conversations between adults when we met relatives or friends.

At weekends, the street became crowded with shoppers, a large number of whom came from surrounding villages and farms. The influx of shoppers gave the town a festive air and I always felt, particularly on summer days when we'd been dressed in clean, freshly-ironed clothes, that we were on a special outing. Most of the shops remained open until eight o'clock on Saturday evening and people were bustling in and out of butchers' and grocers' shops until closing time. In some families, men were not paid their weekly wage until Saturday afternoon and their wives were unable to shop for food until the all-important pay-packet was brought home. Also, some shoppers, especially those of very slim means, waited until the last few minutes to shop, hoping for bargains in perishable goods, items that would not keep until Monday. They were often rewarded for their wait.

A few shops were taken over by new owners during those years, causing a flurry of interest and perhaps a switch of allegiance by some customers to the new businesses. Others paid one or two visits in order to inspect the newly-opened premises and purchased a few token items that may have been a little different or were perhaps unobtainable elsewhere. Most of the old-established businesses however, remained in the same families for many years, passing to succeeding generations.

I loved window-shopping and often dawdled home from school, peering into display windows along the way, deciding what I liked best, whether it be something to wear, to eat, to play with or something I couldn't even use.

The shops my family patronised are particularly remembered: the butcher and baker, the chemist and newsagent, outfitters where our clothes were bought, shoe shops and other establishments where we purchased paint, wallpaper and various household supplies. Some of those, as well as other shops, I remember for reasons that were special to me; perhaps for the personalities of the owners, for specific incidents that occurred therein or because of a certain appeal, even though I may have entered them but rarely during those years.

On our way to school we walked along High Street and although I don't ever recall entering the premises, I vividly remember the leathery, slightly musty smell of LeFevre's saddlery. Interesting items were displayed in the two windows, including horse brasses, leather straps and decorations and the big, flat rolls of coloured braid that we called horse ribbon. Inside the shop, saddles, harness and other large items hung on the walls and the saddler himself sat, often just inside the open door in summer, making or repairing orders for customers.

A little further along the street was one of my favourite shops, Turner's, the pork butcher. My mother bought sausages and other meat there and often, my sister and I were sent on errands to make the purchases. We liked being sent there because we were fascinated by the butcher himself. We had a nickname for him: *Mr Fankoo*! He was a story-book butcher, with a blue and white striped apron tied around his ample waist and wearing a straw boater in summer; in winter he wore a cloth cap. He had a moustache with waxed ends that curled up and was a friendly, jovial man. After he had weighed and wrapped each customer's meat and handed it to them and again upon taking their payment he would say, "Thank you," but due to a slight speech impediment it always sounded like "Fankoo," the second syllable being prolonged slightly. This always delighted us and we liked it when there were several customers to be served ahead of us, so that we could listen to the butcher repeating his "Fankoo" to each customer.

As in most butcher shops in those days, sawdust was strewn on the floor and the shop had an appetising, clean smell. Sausages hung like ropes of elongated, fat pink beads at the rear of one window, behind the display of haslets, faggots, pork pies and always a large, enamel dish of creamy-white pork fat that we called *butchers' lard*, delicious spread on toast or bread and sprinkled lightly with salt. The other window was given over to chops and joints of pork, in the centre of which stood a large dish of *pig's fry*, a popular assortment of liver, kidney and sweetbreads.

With a large knife, Mr. Turner slashed off our pound of sausages from one of the ropes in the window and wrapped them. After receiving our own "Fankoo," my sister and I went off giggling down the street, repeating the word to each other.

A particular incident that occurred one day in Mr. Turner's shop remains with me very clearly. On the day my younger brother was born, when I was eight and a half years old, I was sent there to buy sausages for our dinner. There was one other customer in the shop and I excitedly announced to her and the butcher that I had a new brother, born that day, who weighed eleven pounds. They both roared with laughter and agreed over my head that I had obviously got it all wrong. Mr Turner teased me that he must be a giant. But *they* were wrong and *I* was right; my new brother did indeed weigh eleven pounds.

Next door to the butcher was the chemist's shop, still owned by the same family. One half of the shop was given over to radio sets, gramophones and radio batteries that we called *accumulators*. Cameras and photographic equipment were also sold there and at Christmas, bottles of wine were displayed in the window, old favourites such as Odds On Cocktail, Emu port and Sandeman's sherry. I liked the other part of the shop best, the aroma of soap, perfume, toiletries and medicines assailing the nostrils as one entered.

We shopped there for many items: camphorated oil to rub on our chests when we had colds and prescriptions to be made up after a visit to the doctor; California syrup of figs, that had a delicious taste but was extremely potent; Scott's Emulsion, with the familiar picture on both the bottle label and the outer package of a fisherman with a huge cod over his shoulder; I consumed many bottles of that quite pleasant, though fishy-tasting, creamy emulsion. We also bought Parrish's Food occasionally, a wine-red liquid tonic with an iron content that seemed to shrivel one's mouth. It was supposed to restore strength after an illness. I was sometimes sent to the chemist to buy Woodward's gripe water or Steedman's powders when we had a teething or fretting baby; and I recall too, the scent of Evan Williams shampoo, which we purchased as a powder to be mixed with warm water, usually resulting in a gritty mixture with a few lumps that never completely dissolved; it came in camomile for blonde hair and henna for brunettes. We bought one of each for our family; our hair colours ranged from almost white to extremely dark brown.

Across the street was a bakery that sold crusty, cottage loaves. I'm not sure if they are still made in these mass-produced times; they were a large, round loaf with a much smaller round piece perched on top. The hard, brown crust was an irresistible temptation to small fingers; by the time the loaf arrived home, we'd picked off pieces of crust to nibble along the way.

On hot, summer Sundays, before gas or electric ovens were a common item of household equipment, many housewives took their meat to the bakery to be cooked in the big bread oven for a charge of a penny or two. It was a fairly common sight to see people carrying pans of roast meat, covered by a cloth, hurrying towards their homes just before one o'clock dinner time. The penny or two spent in having the meat roasted at the bakery was probably less than the cost of lighting the coal range to cook it at home. And cook everyone in the family too, on a hot day!

It was from that same bakery we bought our hot cross buns on Good Friday; early in the morning, one of the family walked to the shop to buy the warm yeasty buns, rich with currants and peel. We ate them for breakfast as a traditional treat.

Just past the bakery, where High Street converges on to the market place, stood Kearney's garage; mechanics were busy most of the time repairing cars or other vehicles and there was always an aroma of petrol and oil emanating from the interior. The Kearneys were near neighbours of ours and I remember them as educated and kind people. Once when I was seriously ill, Mrs. Kearney brought me tiny jellies and custards in fish paste jars to tempt my appetite, comics her son had finished with for me to read and pictures pasted on cardboard then cut into jig-saw puzzles to keep me amused. I remember too, the lovely flower garden they grew in front of their house, a riot of colour from low border plants to tall hollyhocks at the back, bordering a fence.

Next to the garage was a fascinating shop run by the Misses Crowson. The two middle-aged ladies were members of Jehovah's Witnesses and besides being somewhat eccentric, were often the butt of a certain amount of derision due to an almost fanatical devotion to their chosen religious beliefs. They were however, always very helpful whenever I went into their shop and I found them rather intriguing, simply because they were different from most other shopkeepers.

Usually I was sent there to buy shoe leather with which my father repaired our shoes, a job he did quite expertly. The pieces of leather, of random shapes and sizes, were stacked on a shelf at the rear of the shop, each piece having the price chalked on it. In addition to leather, the ladies sold most other items required for mending shoes, including rubber soles and heels to be glued or nailed on and cards of metal studs to be hammered into the toes and heels of boys' boots to make the new leather last longer. We girls usually had smaller shoe preservers called *segs* knocked into the heels and we hated them because they made a noise when we walked. Also sold in the shop were shoe laces, narrow as string or wide as ribbon in black, brown or white, in various lengths; and hanging from a rack above the counter, like long strips of brown liquorice, leather laces used for men's' work boots. Tins of *Kiwi* and *Nugget* shoe polish, dubbin for work boots and whitener for canvas summer shoes were displayed beside the boxes of shoe laces.

Another line of merchandise, far removed from shoe repairs, was patent medicines. Prominently displayed were *Carter's Little Liver Pills, Castorets, Parkinson's Pills* and many other such items in demand at the time. Herbal teas were also sold, senna pods and other old-fashioned remedies for digestive and internal disorders. Cough syrups, *Victory V* throat lozenges, boiled sweets and a very potent, bitter liquorice that had an expurgating effect.

The pervading aroma of the shop was of leather, overlaid by a mixture of shoe polish, lozenges and a vague, musty smell reminiscent of rooms that have been closed off for a long time.

Past the war memorial and into Market Street one passed a men's outfitter and an old-fashioned grocery shop from which emanated the odour of brown sugar, cheese, bacon and packing cases before coming to Gray's, owned by the same family for fifty years or more, into the 1980's. It seemed like two shops in one and I remember very clearly the way it was laid out when I used to go in there with my mother. The door opened on to a long, passage-like area with a bricked floor, where household items were displayed; pots and pans, brushes and mops, galvanised baths, tubs and pails, enamel bowls and saucepans etc. Then turning at right angles into the other part of the shop, one was in a confectioner's and tobacconist's with jars of good quality sweets, bars of chocolate, slabs of creamy toffee and fancy boxes of chocolates with pretty pictures on the lids.

I occasionally went there with friends to buy sweets, but rarely bought there myself, as we had a sweet shop in the family. My mother sometimes shopped there for kitchen items and I enjoyed going with her as it was a good excuse to have a look round. I liked shops of all kinds and was always eager to inspect anything from clothing to hardware.

Further along the street, past another men's outfitter, a public house and the cinema, was a bakery with eye-appealing, mouth-watering fancy cakes and pastries displayed in the windows. Often on my way home from school I stopped to press my face against a window, to decide, should I ever have the opportunity, what I would buy. Cream horns, jam tarts, currant buns and chocolate eclairs all vied as favourites, but the *petits fours*, tiny sponge cakes in varying shapes, each in a paper cup, iced and decorated in pastel colours were my final choice.

Many years into the then future, I was to discover that after the 1914-18 war, my father-in-law operated a business as a barber and tobacconist in that very shop. I recall seeing a photograph, taken about 1920, of my parents-in-law and an assistant standing in the doorway of the shop. In 1922 they moved their business to Thorney, where they also became newsagents, vendors of stationery, sweets and fancy goods. Much later, they established a ladies' hairdressing salon, operated by my then future sister-in-law.

At the end of that same side of Market Street stood Mackrell's, in those days one of the town's largest shops. They sold clothing for all members of the family, hats and undergarments, fabric, sewing and knitting requirements and haberdashery. Best of all, at Christmas time they sold toys. A large window at one end of the premises was given over every year for a toy display and as soon as the toys appeared in the window a few weeks before Christmas, we rushed across the corner from school to stand and admire, covet and play the game of choosing which doll, book or toy was "ours". A small side window displayed *Meccano* sets with models of bridges, cranes and so forth, around which boys congregated, but girls stood before the big window to decide which doll they'd like to find beside their bed on Christmas morning.

At the rear of the window were doll prams, cots, tricycles, big teddy bears and other soft toys, while at the front were games and small toys, but it was dolls we mainly discussed. They stood in open, cardboard boxes like little sentries: blondes and brunettes, baby dolls, celluloid dolls - no plastic then - some with hair, others without, some in beautiful dresses, others waiting for their new owners to dress them. The doll that attracted my attention, the one I coveted for two or three consecutive years though never received, was a fairy doll. Displayed in the centre of the window, she too, stood in her little sentry box, elegant in a silver tutu-like dress, a silver band around her golden hair and holding in her tiny, china hand a silver wand with a sparkling star at the end. To me she was the ultimate in dolls at that time, unattainable and perhaps rightly so, for what could one dress a fairy doll in but a fairy dress? One of the pleasures of playing with dolls was to dress and undress them in as many different outfits as possible.

One year there was great excitement as Father Christmas was to appear at the shop. Today it is commonplace to have a Father Christmas in every shopping centre, but it was a new and novel experience for us. A crowd of mothers and children gathered outside on Christmas Eve afternoon, swelling into the road; the few passing buses and cars drove carefully around the crowd. After what seemed an interminable wait, with children growing impatient, an upstairs window finally opened and there, resplendent in red costume and flowing white beard, was the magic gentleman in person. He waved and called out to us, then to our delight released coloured balloons, a few at a time, to float down into our waiting arms. The brightly-coloured, fragile globes were suspended in the late afternoon air, brightening the damp, chill December twilight as children tried to catch them before they floated away, out of reach.

Around the corner from Mackrell's was the Co-op, then a new, multi-department addition to the local shopping scene and a formidable rival to local shopkeepers as the Co-op paid a dividend on every item purchased, claimable twice each year as a cash bonus;

many residents switched allegiance from other shops in order to obtain what came to be known as the *divvy*. In contrast with most of the older shops it seemed light, spacious, shiny and with merchandise attractively displayed.

We sometimes shopped at the clothing department, but never at the grocery, as all our groceries were bought at my grandfather's shop. I recall an amusing incident that occurred one day when I was out shopping with my mother and grandma: the Co-op grocery sold a specialty cake, spongy, light and cream-filled, with pink, white and green layers, cut to the customer's desired weight from a large block of the cake. My grandma wanted to try it, but neither she nor my mother would enter the shop for fear of being "recognised", so they sent me in to buy a pound of the cake while they waited outside. Upon handing me the cake, the assistant asked for my number; I had no idea what she was talking about and stood there, looking puzzled and when asked again, I replied, "Twenty-two", the street number of our house. The assistant said that couldn't be right and I suspect she herself claimed the *divvy* on our cake. We had been allocated a number, but my mother omitted to give it to me when I was sent into the shop. Both she and my grandma laughed heartily when I told them I'd given our house number.

The Co-op was an interesting place because of the pulley system used for transferring money and receipts between the cash office and the various departments. Each customer's money, with the bill for purchases made, was placed in an overhead container that was sent whizzing along cables to a small office where the cashier removed the money, replaced it with the correct amount of change and a receipted bill and sent it flying back to the department where the customer waited. Like a miniature railway, the containers sped all over the premises during busy shopping hours and sometimes became backed up at the cashier's office, so that one had to wait for change to be returned.

My mother bought fabric called Sparva at the Co-op to make summer dresses and other items of clothing for us; it must have been a house brand, as I don't recall it being sold elsewhere. It came in a rainbow of colours and bolts of it were displayed in a window at the beginning of summer, stacked in piles, each colour shown from the palest to the deepest shade. We also bought there a line of children's' underwear with the brand name *Vedonis*, always advertised with the slogan: As worn by the *Vedonis* twins, Bobby and Rita, the label depicting the boy and girl twins showing off their underwear. I wonder if anyone else remembers that; many children of my age must have worn them.

Turning back to Market Street, Johnson's sweet shop stood just around the corner, opposite Mackrell's and conveniently close to the primary school. Mr. Johnson also sold groceries and other items, but we barely noticed those.

Some children I knew had a penny to spend every day on their way to or from school, an undreamed-of luxury for many, myself included. Those children often had older brothers and sisters who worked and provided the pennies, a situation I envied, being the eldest of my family and therefore never on the receiving end of such bounty. Our mother insisted that children who bought sweets every day would grow up to have bad teeth and she may have been right, but that didn't prevent us yearning to have a penny to spend more than once each week. Also, we weren't allowed to spend that penny at Johnson's; it had to be spent at our grandfather's shop because we were told he had better sweets. But it was the "junk" we so longed to buy and occasionally did so, using pennies that could sometimes be earned running errands for neighbours.

I recall items sold in Johnson's that I never saw anywhere else: tiger nuts for instance; wrinkled, brown kernels about the size of a dried pea, with very little flavour. What were they? I have asked many people, but have rarely found anyone who has even heard of them, though I did once read an autobiography in which the author asked the same question, having recalled them from his own boyhood. Then there was Spanish root; dried, brown sticks a few inches long, resembling twigs but which, when one sucked them, separated into bright yellow fibrous strands with a sharp, acid flavour. Sherbert dabs were favourites too and the enormous, cheek-bulging gob-stoppers that changed colour every few minutes and had to be taken out of one's mouth periodically to inspect that phenomenon; they were uncomfortable to eat until their size had diminished and they also prevented coherent speech, but the distorted cheek was part of their attraction.

Before and after school hours and on Saturdays there was a constant stream of children in and out of the shop. Even on Sundays business was brisk, the shop being one of the few to open on the Sabbath, much to the disapproval of some local residents. In summer, delicious ice cream, made on the premises, could be bought there and I have written of that elsewhere.

Heading back towards the market place, past the wallpaper and furniture shop, a cycle shop, a barber's, newsagent's and another garage, one came to Mann's shoe shop. In two small windows, on either side of the door, were displayed shoes for all occasions and all ages: work boots and dress shoes, rubber wellingtons, gym shoes and slippers and tiny baby shoes. Most of our shoes were bought there and I have vivid memories of that little shop. It was part of a very old building and stepping down into it by a steep step was almost like entering a cave. A low ceiling and boxes of shoes lining the walls added to the cave-like atmosphere. Coco matting covered the floor to protect shoes as customers walked back and forth to get the feel of a pair of shoes and inspect them in the floor-level mirrors. Two diminutive, middle-aged ladies attended closely to the business of finding the right shoes to suit each customer.

Sometimes we were sent there on our own to try on a few pairs of shoes which we then took home "on approval" for our parents to choose which pair best suited both *their* purse and *our* feet. Four or five pairs of shoes in boxes were placed on a large square of black cloth that was then tied by the four corners, forming a convenient, though awkward bag in which the shoes could be carried home. At home, we tried on each pair of shoes again, had the ends pressed to make sure there was growing room, then provided more than one pair was suitable, we were given a choice as to which pair we liked best. To me, it sometimes seemed a case of which pair I disliked least; I longed for black patent shoes with ankle straps, but like the fairy doll in the toy shop window, they were unattainable. Our shoes had to be serviceable enough for school, added to which I had a slight foot problem that decreed I must wear shoes with a modicum of support. Having chosen our shoes, we returned the rest, re-wrapped in the black cloth and paid for those we'd kept.

A short distance from the market place, on Whitmore Street, stood Mr. Anthony's barber shop. One of my young uncles served his apprenticeship there and used sometimes to practice his craft on us children on his Thursday half day's holiday. Mr. Anthony was also a photographer and it is in that guise that I remember him best, both from watching him in action and being a subject of his art.

The first recollection I have of facing his camera was when he took a photograph of my sister and myself, aged three and going-on-two, dressed alike in blue velvet dresses. The picture was taken in a studio to the side of the barber shop; it was rather like a conservatory, with lots of glass and natural light and with various props such as small tables, chairs and artificial flowers, used as accents in posing subjects. My sister and I were posed with a chair and a basket of flowers. A few months later, wearing the same dress with a lace collar added, I posed with my mother, grandmother and great-grandparents for a four generations photograph. Mr. Anthony set up his tripod in my grandparents' back yard and after fussing for several minutes to get us all just right, put his head underneath a black cloth, held out a rubber bulb and told us to *watch the birdie*. I still have those two photographs.

A weekly ritual was to walk past Mr. Anthony's shop to view the latest photographs of local weddings and other social events as well as chosen studio portraits of individuals or family groups. They were changed every week and were items of great interest as passers-by stopped to identify people they knew or to admire the dresses in the latest wedding groups.

There were many other shops in the town at that time, but the one I knew best of all was my grandfather's: *H. G. Brown, Grocer and Confectioner*. The shop was located in Eastgate, a stone's throw from the market place; I spent many happy hours in that establishment.

As children, we were given a penny, or if the family budget was tight, a halfpenny to spend on Saturday mornings at Grandpa's shop. The tortuous decision of what to buy in order to obtain maximum value for money was made only after several minutes of considering the contents of the row of sweet jars on the bottom level of the three tiers that displayed the available selection. The cheapest, selling at two pence per quarter pound, were at the bottom, at child's-eye level; the next row contained sweets that cost four pence per quarter pound and the top row displayed the most expensive, at sixpence per quarter. When I was older and helped my grandparents in the shop, I discovered who bought those expensive toffees and chocolates.

While we and other neighbourhood children were deciding whether to buy aniseed balls, hard mixtures, chocolate drops or jelly babies, my grandfather sometimes put on an impromptu act for us, of ventriloquism or musical tricks such as pretending to play an instrument, using only his voice and hands. In his younger days he'd been a member of a group of amateur entertainers and was quite talented in that regard. He played the euphonium in the town band for many years, sang as a church chorister for more than fifty years, and could do unusual things like beating out tunes with bone-handled knives, an accomplishment he'd learned when he'd belonged to a minstrel group, where tunes were played on what were called *bones*. My grandfather liked children and they liked him in return and when he entertained us on Saturday mornings there would often be requests to, "Do that again, Mr. Brown." He mentally stored away the sayings of some of his young customers and repeated them later to his family, chuckling with delight and enjoying them immensely.

When I was old enough I spent many of my Saturdays and some of my holidays helping at the shop. I prepared customers' grocery orders for my grandfather to deliver to neighbouring homes, weighing out sugar, cheese, lard and bacon and assembling the items for each order. Often the lists were written on the backs of used envelopes or other pieces of scrap paper.

On Friday and Saturday evenings young men dressed in their best suits called at the shop for cigarettes and quarter pounds of sweets to eat at *The Pictures*, as our cinema was known; many of them were farm workers from outlying areas with their weekly wages to splurge and I found that it was they who were able to afford the expensive sweets from the top tier of jars. I was kept busy weighing out buttered brazils, sugared almonds, good-quality toffees, cream-filled chocolates and other such delights. Sometimes they bought large, thick bars of Cadbury's chocolate or even small boxes of good chocolates, the latter being especially popular if they were out to impress a girl.

I came to know the price of everything: groceries, sweets, tobacco and cigarettes, patent medicines and cough lozenges, pencils and notebooks, bundles of fire kindling, shoe laces, cleaning supplies and so on. There were times when I was convinced I could happily spend the rest of my life serving customers in that little shop; it became almost a second home.

To this day, when I wrap food for my freezer I do so exactly as my grandfather taught me all those years ago when I wrapped lard and cheese in sheets of grease proof paper; and I'm certain I could still deftly shake down brown or white sugar in thick, blue bags and fold down the tops the way I was taught.

The shop was demolished several years ago, some time after my grandparents had departed their earthly life, to make way for a block of flats, many of them occupied by seniors. I think they would have approved of that.

* * * * *

SOCIALISING AND CELEBRATING

Most families we knew had to budget carefully in order to keep up a reasonable standard of living or in a very few cases, simply to survive, so there was little spare cash to spend on a social whirl, however modest. Consequently, most groups and organisations in the town were well attended and supported, giving adults, adolescents and children an opportunity to participate in social activities. In addition to the always-popular Girl Guides, Brownies, Boy Scouts and Cubs, there were youth groups affiliated with churches, music lessons for those whose parents were able to afford them, and for girls, dancing classes where budding Shirley Temples tap-danced away in patent leather shoes and short frilly skirts.

Dedicated leaders of the various groups devoted many hours of their time to provide young people with outlets for their energy and creativity and we in turn enjoyed both the participation in programs devised to keep us occupied and the contact with other young people in an environment that was both social and companionable, yet still sufficiently structured to satisfy our competitive spirit. We looked forward to the weekly meetings, rarely missing them however inclement the weather. Since we had no television or other such devices to entertain us at home, we were accustomed to filling many of our leisure hours in outside pursuits.

We trekked out in rain and fog, frost and heat to play organised team games, sing rousing campfire songs, learn how to send messages in Morse code or signal them in semaphore and spend hours tying knots we would seldom, if ever use, except perhaps the reef knot. During the summer months we spread out into local fields and spinneys to track each other along trails by means of arrows chalked on trees, sticks arranged in patterns on the ground and other such ingenious devices that, unless we one day found ourselves exploring jungles and forests, would be of no future use to us. Or, like Hansel and Gretel leaving their trail of crumbs, we scattered tiny pieces of paper along a paper chase route, hoping they wouldn't blow away before the rest of the pack managed to track us to a pre-arranged *rendezvous*.

We were expected, in our family, to take part in such activities, to sing in church choirs and generally become involved in school and community groups. I needed no encouragement and belonged to several organisations, beginning with Brownies and ending with a teen drama group.

Some of the my clearest recollections of social activities outside my home are of the very earliest ones. Once involved in the mainstream of school life, social experiences tend to fuse in the memory as a *mélange* of meetings, parties, games, sports and camping trips spread over several years and sometimes difficult to separate. But when we are very young, every experience is an event of some importance, either a singular occurrence or a regularly-attended gathering; as we grow older, we often seem to recall those early experiences with great clarity.

I can recall a single incident of the 1926 general strike, when I was just two years old. It is a brief, but vivid memory of being among a large crowd on a railway station platform late at night. My father held me, while my mother held my baby sister. We'd been on a day trip to the seaside, as I discovered many years later and upon arriving at the station, found a crowd of people but no train. Eventually, after a very long wait, a train arrived to take us home. Of the journey I recall nothing, but have a clear recollection of looking over the heads of the people in the crowd from my father's shoulder.

My first regular social outing remains very clear. Each Tuesday afternoon my mother took us to the infant welfare centre. I was perhaps three or four years old when we began attending *The Welfare*, as the centre was known; it was primarily a clinic where mothers could have babies and pre-school children weighed, checked for specific or general health problems and seek medical advice. A doctor and nurse were in attendance. It was also a social outing for the mothers; they had few expectations of outings or expeditions involving expense, so those who needed both the stimulation and relaxation of contact with other like-minded contemporaries, supported and took advantage of such groups.

It was held in one of the church halls and after the clinical segment of the afternoon had been completed, mothers sat in a semi-circle drinking tea, sharing the latest news and enjoying a good gossip while we children played with our Tuesday friends, sometimes, admittedly, becoming little too boisterous.

A generation later, some of us who had played together as children met in that same hall with our own babies, taking them as we ourselves had been taken by our mothers, for medical check-ups and to purchase bottles of orange juice concentrate for a few pennies. We also bought National Dried Milk for our babies, for we had a war behind us by then and baby foods had been nationalised by the government to ensure the good health of war time and post-war babies.

In addition to attending weekly meetings of almost any group there were bonuses in the form of Christmas parties, summer outings and camping trips. Christmas parties began with the annual *Welfare* party when we were very young, with a doctor dressed up as Father Christmas, dispensing gifts from a tree almost as tall as the room; at least it seemed as tall as that to small children. We ate thin bread and butter, jellies and trifles and played simple, age-old games such as Oranges and Lemons. At Brownie and Girl Guide parties the games were more boisterous, allowing us to let off steam as we egged our teams on. Sometimes there were fancy dress contests, with small prizes. After tea at the annual Sunday School party, prizes were awarded for attendance during the preceding year. They were always books, though not always, as I recall, suitable for our ages. I suspect attention was sometimes paid to quantity rather than quality, due to the limited funds available. However, the books were all read eventually, as we "grew into them".

A social occasion popular with all age groups was that most English of summer events, the garden fete. Our church, like most others, held an annual fete that varied barely at all from year to year in content and format; part of the garden fete's charm and attraction was its timeless traditions.

Held on a Thursday afternoon, the fete was staged in the vicarage gardens against a backdrop of trees, shrubs, lawns and rose gardens. For several weeks prior to the fete, church workers planned the fund-raising stalls and competitions and arranged for volunteers to be responsible for each one. An invitation was extended to a personage of some prestige in the district to officially open the fete and a temporary dais was erected upon which the vicar and his wife, the invited guests and other church officials were to sit for the opening ceremony. A small girl was chosen to present a bouquet to the invited lady and another to present a boutonniere for the lapel of the most important male guest. I always longed to be chosen to present the bouquet, to climb the steps to the dais and bob a curtsey as I handed over the flowers, but I never did achieve that honour. One year my sister did and I watched enviously as she made the presentation wearing a blue silk dress and head-hugging straw bonnet trimmed with blue ribbon.

We treated the garden fete as a dress-up occasion and wore our Sunday clothes, complete with straw hat if it was a warm day. The ladies on the dais wore wide-brimmed, summery hats and formal dresses and after a few brief speeches in their clear, cultured voices, the garden fete was declared open.

The vicar's wife led the official party on a tour of the stalls to purchase a few items here and there, often from the "White Elephant" stall. They must have amassed quite a collection of trinkets as they made their annual round of district fetes. Perhaps they eventually donated them to their own church fetes to be re-sold.

With a penny or two to spend, we made a beeline for the bran tub, a feature that as far as I can recall was in evidence at every garden fete I attended. In a barrel filled with bran or sawdust were buried small parcels, attractively wrapped, and approximately to the value of the penny or two that was the cost of delving into the barrel as deeply as possible, hoping the best things were at the bottom. It was like giving oneself a present. Usually the parcels contained very ordinary items such as tiny toys, books, whistles or games, but it was the surprise element that was fun.

I'm certain that fund-raising projects popular at those fetes were of the type that still endure at such events: stalls selling crocheted, knitted, embroidered and other needlework items; cakes, jams and other kitchen delicacies; a White Elephant stall; darts to throw at dart boards, balls into pails, hoops around stakes in the ground, and other such games of manual skill. There were competitions to guess the number of marbles or buttons in a jar, the weight of a cake or the name of a doll, the item in question being the prize for the most accurate guess.

It was all so leisurely and timeless; men wore their best suits, ladies in summery hats and silky dresses sipped tea and ate fancy sandwiches and cakes in the refreshment tent and people walked around the garden to admire the flowers and talk to friends they met along the way. There was an air of formality, of being among people of importance; it was in a sense our substitute for upper class garden parties and resembled to a degree the tranquil days before The Great War when the Edwardians and the early Georgians thought their world would last forever as they drifted through endless garden parties, boating regattas, balls and weekend house parties. Looking back, those were peaceful, happy times when we were innocent of what was to face us within a few years.

For adolescents and adults, in addition to belonging to organisations, there were whist drives, socials and dances, held mainly during the winter months. Dances were held in a large hall known as The Public Hall and I recall standing outside with friends to watch evening-gowned ladies and their escorts make their entrances. The escorts I ignored, but longed for the day when I'd be old enough to wear a long, elegant gown and perhaps attend such a function. But when I *was* old enough we were in the midst of a war and along with my contemporaries I danced happily to swingy music wearing short skirts and clumsy, war time shoes, often with bare legs to save precious stockings. Our partners wore Army, Air Force or Naval uniform, or perhaps the uniforms of Allied countries. It would be several years before long evening gowns were worn again.

We looked forward to seasonal holidays and celebrations, seeing them as a break in routine, neatly dividing the year into sections, each holiday bringing its customs and traditions and each one also taking us one step closer to the most important of them all: Christmas, the culmination of our year.

We didn't celebrate a New Year's holiday, but a few traditions were observed, the most important being the custom of "first-footing". It was held to be good luck if a dark man was the first to cross the threshold on the first day of the year, bringing with him bread and coal, signifying food and warmth. My father was dark-haired and though he wasn't normally a superstitious person, I remember his going outside just before midnight on New Year's Eve, then re-entering as soon as the new year arrived, the ritual lump of coal and loaf of bread in his hands, ensuring our good fortune for the coming year.

Easter was the first holiday of the year to be celebrated. It was perceived as the beginning of summer, though the weather didn't always co-operate in that regard. On Good Friday morning we ate freshly-baked hot cross buns for breakfast, split and buttered, a real treat. Sunday was, as now, the religious holiday and special services were held in churches of all denominations. When we were young, our mother attended an early morning communion service, leaving us all in bed, a rare treat for her. We eagerly awaited her return, as she brought us each a chocolate egg from our grandfather's shop, having called there on her way home. As soon as we heard her come into the house, we rushed to meet her and claim our eggs.

Easter Sunday was also the traditional day for wearing new spring outfits and many of the female population kept a wary eye on the weather during preceding days. If the day turned out cool and blustery, they held on to their new hats and suffered the cold in flimsy new dresses. A fine, sunny day was a bonus, adding to the colourful effect of the bright, summery clothes. In our family, if we needed new outfits at that time of year, we always kept them to be worn for the first time at Easter.

The other summer holidays, Whitsun and August Bank Holiday, both now changed since those days were spent by many people at local sporting events, excursions to the seaside or elsewhere, or just relaxing at home to enjoy an extra day off.

We looked forward to Guy Fawkes day on November 5th; Bonfire Day, we always called it, a celebration of the day in 1605 when Guy Fawkes and his fellow conspirators tried to blow up the Houses of Parliament. Each year we burned Guy's effigy on a bonfire of hoarded rubbish, cheering when he collapsed into the flames. Before lighting the bonfire we let off fireworks; it was often a foggy, cold or rainy evening, so we dressed in layers of warm clothing. Catherine Wheels, nailed to fence posts, spun round and showered sparks in all directions; Roman Candles hissed coloured streams of light into the darkness; and Golden Rain evoked *oohs* and *aahs* as the jets of sparkly light curved up in graceful arcs, then fell, dying, to the ground. They were over far too soon. Around the bonfire we held sparklers in our hands and watched rockets from neighbouring yards zoom into the air. After the bonfire and the guy had been reduced to ashes we went into the house for a cup of hot cocoa before going to bed. As we lay there, we could hear the hiss of rockets, often being let off by youths who lived next door to us, and the subsequent bangs as coloured stars exploded into the air, illuminating the sky.

Christmas was the holiday we most looked forward to, as children still do all over the Christian world. We discussed it for weeks beforehand, peering into shop windows, coveting toys we were not likely to receive, but hoping and dreaming all the same.

Outside butcher shops, geese, ducks, chickens and perhaps an occasional turkey hung by their feet, wings drooping, a frieze of coloured feathers edged with a fringe of yellow and orange beaks. We plucked and cleaned our own poultry then, the eviscerated birds so familiar today being unknown to us; but the good flavour of freshly-killed poultry is now almost extinct.

We had a small Christmas tree, small enough to fit into a large flower pot. It was never decorated until Christmas Eve and I remember the excitement I felt the first year I was considered old enough to stay up late and help decorate it. The tree may have been small, but we thought it beautiful. Firs, pines and spruces do not grow profusely, as they do in my adopted country and large trees were very expensive, usually seen during my childhood only at public parties, in large halls. We owned some pretty tree decorations that had survived from my mother's childhood and each year they were carefully unpacked from their tissue paper bed in a box that was stored from year to year on a high shelf in a cupboard. There were delicate glass swans with feathery tails and coloured glass balls covered with a fine, silvery mesh; and tiny coloured boxes in unusual shapes, originally having held chocolates, that hung by silky cords and still contained the original packing in which the chocolates had nestled. My youngest nieces and nephews hung the survivors of those same decorations on their tree, the third generation to do so.

We also decorated our homes with paper streamers and evergreens, our version of "decking the halls". Streamers were hung in loops across the ceiling, sometimes with a balloon or two for added effect. Holly, laurel, fir, box and mistletoe could be bought at florist shops, but we, strange though it may appear, bought ours at the cemetery. The caretaker lived in a house just inside the cemetery gates and at Christmas he pruned off excessive growth from the many evergreens that grew in the cemetery and sold the resulting boughs to nearby residents. The outdoors-y scent of the freshly-cut greenery permeated the house as we tucked it behind pictures and mirrors and hung a traditional sprig of mistletoe in a doorway.

During the last week or so at school before Christmas we messily glued strips of glossy, coloured paper into long chains to decorate classrooms, made Christmas cards that were often equally messy and completed gifts in handicraft classes. We sang carols, listened to the story of the Nativity and sometimes acted it out for parents and friends.

Going to bed on Christmas Eve was anticipation, insomnia and a determination to stay awake until *He* had been. Father Christmas came right into our bedrooms and after filling stockings, left larger gifts either at the foot of our beds or on the floor beside them. Most beds had wooden, metal or brass ends, so there was usually a handy knob on which to hang a stocking. Despite our resolution not to, we did of course fall asleep. On awaking, we immediately peered at the end of the bed for the reassuring, knobbly shapes of stockings outlined against the first light of dawn, then groped with our feet or leaned over to look on the floor for a box or book or game. Our toys were not gift-wrapped, but were placed in our bedrooms unwrapped except for the boxes in which they may have been purchased.

In our stockings we found the traditional orange and nuts, perhaps a small book or toy and almost always a pink or white sugar mouse. I don't recall seeing sugar mice after the war, but during our childhood they were synonymous with Christmas, either as a stocking stuffer or hung on the tree, to be eaten after the tree was dismantled. We received one large gift, usually a doll, book, game or other toy. Sometimes we received chocolates or sweets from unmarried aunts and uncles and usually a small gift from grandparents. Small bounty compared to the number of gifts given to today's children; even so, we were often reminded by our parents that we received far more than they did as children. Perhaps each generation of parents believes that to be true of its offspring.

Christmas dinner was more often than not a large cockerel, fattened up on a local farm or in one's own back yard. Some families had duck or goose but turkey was unknown to us, being both rare and expensive in those days. We rarely ate chicken at any other time of year; it was not the inexpensive, mass-produced meat common today. Lots of sage and onion stuffing accompanied the chosen bird, the sage freshly-picked from our own garden. No Christmas dinner was complete without Christmas pudding, sometimes called plum pudding, and it too, had its traditions. Tiny, silver charms or silver threepenny coins were hidden in the pudding and great care was taken when apportioning it to ensure each of the children received a charm or "threepenny joey" on their plate. A sweet, white sauce was served with the pudding.

Most families gathered with relatives for a celebration Christmas tea and an evening of cards, games and carol singing and we did that too, at the home of our maternal grandparents, where there were also several young uncles with their girl friends and wives and later, a few cousins. Most of my cousins however, arrived when I was in my teens or older. Before beginning tea we pulled crackers, wore the party hats they contained and read out the silly jokes. The high-light of tea time, after wafer-thin bread and butter, tinned fruit with tinned cream and mince pies, was a rich fruit cake, covered first with a thick layer of marzipan, over which was a hard, white icing. Tiny robins and snowmen perched on the icing and a festive, paper frill was pinned around the cake.

After tea we sang carols, accompanied by Grandma on the piano and along with the carols we always insisted on singing, *John Brown's body lies a'mouldering in the grave*, because John Brown was the name of one of our uncles. Chestnuts were roasted in the fire while we cracked almonds, brazils and barcelonas. Sometimes we children were allowed a sip of port, very grown up and daring! At some point during the evening my grandfather prepared a treat called *snapdragon*, that I don't recall seeing or hearing of elsewhere. Raisins were spread on a large platter, brandy poured over them and ignited, then with the light out we watched the tiny blue flames lick at the raisins before eating them, picking them off the dish with our fingers. They were delicious.

The evening usually ended with each person receiving a small gift, produce from a snowman made of cardboard covered with cotton wool. The snowman was brought out every year and filled with gifts by Grandma. I recall one summer day, when I was helping her to clean a bedroom cupboard, coming across the snowman and thinking how tawdry and out of place he looked among the stashed-away junk; but the following Christmas he seemed white and seasonal as ever with his black top hat dusted off and his felt eyes and mouth straightened for his annual appearance.

We never wanted to go home, protesting, even as we drooped with tiredness, that we weren't really sleepy; we longed for the warmth and conviviality of the family gathering to last for ever. But the next day we woke up remembering our new toys and rushed downstairs to spend the whole day playing with them, blissfully happy, Christmas Day already a memory.

* * * * *

PASTIMES AND PLAYTIMES

Home entertainment today means television, VCRs, radio, stereo records and tapes, video games, home computers and sophisticated educational toys, in addition to the traditional board games and cards. Simply naming some of those now common pastimes reminds us that as children our vocabulary didn't even contain the words that describe them. Stereo ... computer ... television ... video ... they were alien words, barely invented at that time.

Radio was a new and innovative medium in communications to my generation of children. I recall my uncles experimenting with cat's whisker sets and their placing a headphone on me so that I could listen to the distorted voices of singers and announcers crackling over the air waves. Reception was often poor, but we considered it miraculous. Gradually, wireless sets, as they were known, began to appear in many homes, though ownership was by no means universal during those early years, a parallel with television a generation later.

Radio intrigued me. Although we didn't own a set for several years, my grandparents did and I took advantage of every opportunity to listen in, often on Saturday evenings, when we usually visited them for an hour or two, after the weekend shopping was done. I recall hearing a weekly program from London called *In Town Tonight*, its signature tune the popular *Knightsbridge March*; well-known personalities were interviewed, though I cannot now recall the name of the interviewer. I do remember being fascinated by listening to stars from show business and other persons of importance talking about their lives and the reasons why they were in London at that time. My childhood interest in that and similar programs developed into an adult interest in biographies. A variety hour followed *In Town Tonight:* we heard all the popular music hall performers of the day, most of whom were beginning to extend their careers from the stage into the new medium of radio, giving them country-wide exposure and often becoming household names. Stanley Holloway, Wee Georgie Wood, Jack Warner, Elsie and Doris Waters, Jeanne de Casselais, Cardew "The Cad" Robinson and many, many more became well-known to everyone who listened to the wonderful new entertainment medium.

How else did we entertain ourselves? After tea on winter evenings, with a good fire blazing in the coal range, we settled down to amuse ourselves around the big, solid table that stood in the centre of the room. The lamp, placed on the table, radiated its mellow light over us, leaving the rest of the room in a half light that cast shadows on the walls, large and grotesque, to follow us each time we moved. The table itself sometimes figured in our games: draped with an old blanket it became a playhouse, shop, castle or animal cage and was even turned upside down sometimes to became a ship, a broom handle tied to one leg for a mast.

Mostly though, we sat around the table on winter evenings to play cards, dominoes, snakes and ladders or other board games. Our father often joined in the games and indeed, taught us most of the card and domino games while Mother sat to one side, knitting, mending or darning. We played gambling games, using a box of buttons for money, but it didn't turn us into adult gamblers or card players, except to play with our own children and grandchildren.

For a change, we sometimes drew pictures or practised our writing and spelling on the insides of used, opened-up envelopes, or we read books and comics. One winter, someone gave us a fascinating modelling material called *glitter-wax;* in pastel colours, with tiny gold and silver flecks throughout, the wax was cleaner and prettier than plasticine and could be formed into models that kept their shape better too. The drawback was that being wax it took a great deal of manipulation before it was pliable enough to use and often had to be softened for us by our father. He enjoyed modelling too and could make very life-like animals and other objects; he had great manual dexterity and during his retirement made beautiful rugs and stitched needlepoint kneelers for one of the churches. One Christmas when my brother received a fretwork kit, then a popular gift for boys, it was Father's fingers that itched to saw around the design on the fragile wood and assemble the models. He often patched his own work clothes when our mother was busy and a very good job he made of it too! He also amused us by making shadow pictures with his hands, the light from the table lamp casting the shadows on to the dark blue window blind. Rabbits, birds and other animals appeared on the blind, waggling their ears or flapping wings. Father could be a difficult man and at times a stern disciplinarian, but there was also a playful aspect to his character; in retrospect, I think he enjoyed our toys and games because they represented a lack of such items in his own boyhood. He was also very proud of his children, though he would never have admitted that!

Being a large family, there were just enough of us to play boisterous games like musical chairs, oranges and lemons and other games we made up; music was by courtesy of an old, wind-up gramophone. One invented game was a variation on musical chairs: how it began is lost to memory, but due to a specific incident that occurred on one occasion we played the game, it remains firmly entrenched in family lore. To play, we sat in a semi-circle around the fire with one player minus a chair; we each chose the name of a well-known railway station, then the person standing, called out "All change, London and York" or whichever stations were chosen. The two players called had to exchange chairs while at the same time the chair-less player attempted to sit down in one of their chairs; if he or she did so, then a new person was *It*. One evening when we decided to play, our younger brother, then about two years old, wanted to join in. We argued he was too young, but our parents insisted he be allowed to play; when asked which station he wanted to represent, he created one of those family jokes that last for years by replying, "Cocoa". We almost fell off our chairs with laughter while Little Brother, unaware he'd said something funny and upset at being laughed at, sat with tears oozing from his big, blue eyes. He refused to be a proper station, despite our many suggestions, so we had to call, "All change, London and Cocoa"; each time the word was called, we dissolved into hysterical giggles. It became part of the game and Cocoa was one of our regular stations after that. Inevitably, we sometimes argued about whose turn it was to be the Cocoa station.

We never did discover why Little Brother wanted so badly to be Cocoa, though it was his favourite bedtime drink. He was highly amused when I recounted the incident to him many years later, he not having remembered it at all. Obviously his psyche hadn't been permanently damaged by the ridicule he suffered at the hands of his older brother and sisters.

During our childhood there were few automatic record players. Large and cumbersome *radiograms* were beginning to appear on the home music scene, but for the most part, records were played on wind-up gramophones, older ones sometimes having a trumpet-shaped speaker attached. Long playing records were a rarity; most had only one song or piece of music on each side and so had to be changed or flipped over frequently. We considered the system quite sophisticated, however. We owned an old gramophone bequeathed to us by one of our young uncles when he bought a new, more up to date model and we derived hours of pleasure from playing our few records, most of them also donated by our uncles when they became tired of them or they acquired cracks and other flaws. A line of a song repeated over and over became part of the entertainment, as did allowing the gramophone to slow down by not winding it, or by altering the speed so that singers either drawled so slowly they appeared to be going to sleep or they sounded like chattering animals in animated cartoons. Lively marches could be adjusted to sound funereal and a crack in a record played at high speed gave the singer hiccups.

Occasionally during the summer holidays we were allowed to take the gramophone outside and since we played all the records regardless of the type of music, it must sometimes have startled neighbours and tradesmen to hear Christmas carols issuing forth on a hot August day. Our selection varied from carols to comedy, marches, cowboy songs and a few of Gracie Field's hits. She was a great favourite both with us and our parents.

On winter or rainy days we spent hours cutting up paper. All we needed was a pile of old newspapers or magazines and scissors - with warnings regarding their use - and we settled down to cut and fold, often sitting on the hearth rug in front of the fire. We made face masks and funny hats, table mats and even table cloths from whole pages of newspaper; we cut out people from adverts and clothes to fit on them, like commercial cut-out dolls. Our paper creations survived for a few days, after which time they were gathered up and burned on the fire.

Sometimes our scissors were put to a more practical use as we were kept busy cutting up old clothing and left-over materials to make hearth rugs; the material was first cut into narrow strips, then into short lengths. It was fun in some respects, deciding which colours to use for the border and which for the centre design. We grumbled when the fabric was thick and scissors dug into our fingers, but we admired the new rug when it was completed. It was an exercise in recycling. In the thirties we did so out of necessity; later, in the forties, when war time shortages forced everyone to recycle, we'd had plenty of practice.

When winter was over and daylight hours stretched into the evening, children spilled out into the streets to play after tea.

During the spring and summer months we enjoyed many of the games children still play; the lore of play changes slowly. We skipped with ropes to tunes still heard today, played hopscotch on chalked-out squares, bowled wooden hoops, bounced balls to catchy rhymes or played rounders with them. Boys played football or cricket, bowled iron hoops, whipped tops along the street or joined the girls in co-ed games.

We looked forward to the summer holidays, visualising them as endless days of play and pleasure. As children of all generations have done, we engaged in complicated pretend games with our friends; we set up shops, using empty boxes and tins from our mother's kitchen for supplies and chalked out rooms on the ground for a school, with a few books, pencils and paper to furnish them. Occasionally it all became so involved that we argued heatedly, causing some of the children to sweep off with their toys in anger or tears, effectively ending the game.

We wrote and acted plays. Dressing up was ever popular and in addition to making use of cast-off clothing, we made costumes from penny rolls of coloured crepe paper, spending hours cutting and sewing dresses that rarely fitted and consequently split at the seams when we tried them on. But we packed them away in boxes and rehearsed the plays that were liberally cast with princes and princesses, fairies and elves. With no television to prod us into space, monster or other such adventures, our imaginations lacked sophistication. For the performance of our dramatic efforts we made tickets from pieces of paper, and the audience, consisting of other children, sat on boxes to watch the play. Because some of our costumes didn't fit, we persuaded our mothers to allow us to wear our best dresses; we embellished them with crepe paper flowers and cloaks and transformed ourselves into royalty with cardboard crowns covered with silver and gold foil from cigarette packets.

Later in the summer we spent an afternoon or two blackberrying along country roads close to home, armed with jam jars to hold the luscious fruit. Always, it seemed, the largest and ripest berries grew tantalisingly out of reach at the top of a hedge or on the far side of a wide ditch filled with water or prickly wild rose bushes. It was however, a delightful way in which to idle away a late summer afternoon, despite the lack of productivity at the end of it. Inevitably we found other interesting things to see and do as we carried out our half-hearted search for blackberries. Boys searched for birds' nests in hedgerows; we picked wild flowers and sat on the grass to make daisy chains for our hair and with no grown-ups to deter us, ran and skipped in the dustiest places. A diversion was to climb on field gates and shout at cows to make them run away, or sneak into grain fields to pick ears of wheat to chew as we dawdled along. Boys captured insects and imprisoned them in match boxes that they always seemed to carry and we talked and argued and held serious discussions on many topics, about which we often knew nothing.

Trim houses and bungalows with neat front gardens now stand where we scuffed along in the gravel and dust on those endless, summer afternoons.

The few berries that remained in the bottom of our jars when we reached home were almost shaken to a pulp, the rest having been eaten along the way, as our mouths and fingers testified. There were usually enough though, to mix with cooking apples to make a delicious pudding in a suet crust for our dinner the following day.

On other afternoons we carried a picnic tea to *The Rec*, our local recreation grounds, where swings, a see-saw and a small roundabout were the main attractions. With sandwiches and a bottle of lemonade or ginger beer packed in a shopping bag we set off early with instructions to stay there until after tea time. But we never lasted that long: by four o'clock we'd eaten our sandwiches and decided it was time to return home, where we found our parents enjoying a quiet meal on their own and non too pleased to see us back, hungry and ready to eat all over again.

Some days I liked to sit in a sunny corner and read, or just dream time away. One such day seems magical in retrospect. I'd been dawdling along a river bank with some friends, inspecting tadpole and insect life at the edge of the water, when I decided to lie down and rest, wanting to be on my own. Although it happened so long ago, I still have a vivid recollection of lying there perfectly still, hidden in the long, dry grasses that grew in abundance. Ears of wild oats and barley were at eye level, papery, scarlet poppies splashing them with colour; through the long stalks I watched the sky, brilliantly blue and flecked with puffy little white clouds that moved lazily, changing shape as they drifted along. Butterflies settled and swayed on the grasses and insects droned around my head. From the nearby railway a goods train chugged along, its trucks rattling across a wooden bridge. It was one of those rare, remembered moments that flash into one's mind like a coloured slide projected on a screen, complete in every detail. I can almost hear the rustle of the grass, feel the heat and hear the sounds of that perfect summer afternoon.

One of the town's tennis courts was located very close to our house and although we didn't understand the game, we loved to watch, sitting outside the high, wire fence that surrounded the court. We were intrigued by the players in their immaculate, white outfits and by the strange-sounding scores. Some days tournaments were held, with players from other clubs competing, creating a festive, garden-party air. Doctors and other professional people were the regular players and to us they belonged to a world quite alien to the one we lived in. Class distinction didn't really begin to disappear until the war levelled us to a large degree by the stringencies of everyday life and by the suffering that struck both the humble and the great among us.

Those were magical years, the good times remembered, the not-so-good days obliterated by time. Like most of our friends during those years, we owned few toys and received very little pocket money, but our imaginations ran riot and knew no bounds. It is the things we *did* rather than the things we *had* that have stood the test of time, from cosy winter evenings playing games around a fireside to long summer days spent in outdoor play. With each passing year those days recede further into the past, yet become more clearly remembered.

* * * * *

ENTERTAINMENT

In the present era of family cars, good public transportation and comparative affluence, many people travel, often long distances, to enjoy sophisticated entertainment in cities and large towns. First-rate musicals, operas, the latest films and the newest plays are all within reach of most people; in addition, fans travel the country, the continent and the world to watch national and international sporting events.

It was not always so. Until the second world war changed almost everyone's life style, entertainment for many small town residents was often home produced. True, there was a good-sized city only seven miles distant from our town and during our childhood a new theatre and a new cinema were built there. More people then began to travel the short distance to see up-to-date films or to patronise the Embassy, the new theatre. Variety shows were staged there, with well-known music hall artistes, an occasional good play and always, at Christmas, a pantomime. There was also a small repertory theatre where a new play was staged each week by a group of dedicated actors and actresses, many of whom became well-known locally.

Nonetheless, for the majority of families, entertainment meant the local cinema, amateur concerts, plays and other such events. Most of them were anticipated with pleasure, each production being discussed beforehand and analysed afterwards as seriously as though we were all media critics. The actors' performances were either lauded or criticised and individual acts assessed. We took great interest in our local actors: professional actors and actresses were anonymous or distant personalities; our performers were real people whom we knew as teachers, parents, shop assistants or in other everyday occupations.

Audiences arrived early at concerts in order to ensure a good view of the stage. Seated on hard chairs in the Legion Hall or a church hall, we found the atmosphere as exciting as we now find it to relax in comfortable seats in a real theatre, waiting for the show to commence. The dimming of lights in the hall, the brightly-lit stage, the curtains finally parting or rising to reveal the first act, costumed actors and actresses and the unfolding of plots or rousing choruses was far removed from real life and we gave the performance our full attention. We particularly watched for friends and relatives to appear

in their roles, while fond parents and grandparents looked on proudly
as their offspring delivered their lines, tap-danced, recited or sang.
Dressed as animals, flowers, kings and queens, fairies, elves or
shepherds, children were forgiven mistakes. In fact, a departure from
planned business or a sudden dry-up as someone forgot their lines and
looked to a prompter in the wings, was perceived as inevitable. It was
all part of the show, although adult actors were not so easily forgiven.

In most audiences every strata of local society was represented. A
segment of the affluent *élite*, usually those associated with the
evening's performing group; relatives and friends of those taking part;
avid concert-goers who attended everything; appreciative patrons who
genuinely enjoyed amateur productions and believed in supporting
them; the young, middle-aged and elderly and sometimes a small
nuisance element of young people who sat at the back of the hall and
interrupted the performance with deprecating remarks or occasional
catcalls, more from collective bravado than a real objection to what
was happening on stage.

As a child I was several times behind the footlights, usually acting
a role in a play. I was sometimes given major roles, partly due to
having a good memory and therefore unlikely to forget my lines,
could project my voice and also, for some reason, had a stage
presence. That fact seems odd to me in retrospect, as I was a timid
and withdrawn child in most respects; but with hindsight, I think I
probably enjoyed the "showing off" aspect of acting. It was a
legitimate method of being someone else, of acting in a ridiculous,
tragic or exaggerated manner without being reprimanded and being
able to make people laugh, cry or applaud. I loved it and still
remember the elation savoured at the time and recalled for days
afterwards.

At that time there was an annual, national Boy Scout show known
as *The Gang Show*. Similar shows were produced all over the country
and our local troop followed suit. The show traditionally got off to a
rollicking start with all the Scouts and Cubs on stage singing with
gusto and enjoyment the Gang Show signature tune, *We're Riding
Along On The Crest Of A Wave* behind blue, cut-out cardboard waves
that "flowed" along the front of the stage. A series of short skits,
tableaux, comedy acts and take-offs of popular radio shows made up
the performance and kept the audience on the edge of their seats,

interested, laughing and applauding. The boys had a great time dressing up in outlandish costumes, the biggest laughs always evoked when they were cast in female roles.

Our family was interested in Boy Scout activities as at that time we lived next door to a family whose three sons were keen Scouts. Their home was an unofficial meeting place for a large segment of the troop and as a small girl I often peered through the fence in fascination at the good-natured gang in their dashing Baden-Powell hats and uniforms adorned with rows of badges as they horsed around with each other. All of them, within a few years of that happy time, served in the armed forces; some did not return, including one of our then neighbours. When I remember those young men, I see them not as uniformed servicemen, or even as adult civilians, but as carefree teenagers in Boy Scout uniforms, enjoying their activities to the full.

The Sunday School I attended staged an annual concert comprising two plays, one performed by the teachers, the other by the children. Our Sunday School superintendent produced the children's' play and in order to practice their lines together, the cast met at his home one or two evenings each week. He was a shoe repairer by trade and we assembled in his cramped little workshop among the boots and shoes, nails and lasts, with the smell of leather and shoe dye in our nostrils. To this day, when I enter a shoe repair shop I am reminded of those long ago play rehearsals.

Entertainment also took place out of doors during the summer months, the annual sports day being a favourite with many people. It was held in a field at the edge of the town, a field long since built over by a post-war housing estate. Then, it seemed almost like going into the country. A parade through the town often preceded the sporting events, with both children and adults competing in fancy dress contests, as well as children on decorated bicycles or wheeling decorated dolls' prams, all competing for prizes to be awarded later in the day.

At the sports field, families staked out their preferred site from which to watch the fun. Races were held for all age groups, beginning with the youngest children and progressing to adults by early evening. Running races, egg and spoon, three-legged and sack races were run off, causing hilarity among both competitors and spectators. A popular event was the slow bicycle race, in which contestants attempted to reach the finishing line *last*, wobbling along as their bicycles veered from side to side, riders trying to remain mounted while at the same time moving ever so slowly along the course. Competitors in every event were cheered and encouraged by onlookers as though they were striving for an Olympic medal. Adults puffed and panted along, probably not having run in a race since the previous year, but determined to show how fit and athletic they were. Or thought they were! There was often a special attraction later in the evening, perhaps a group of motorcyclists performing stunts that thrilled the spectators or some years an equestrian event.

The day's finale was always a tug-of-war contest between local firms. The participants flexed their muscles and dug in their heels as they strived to pull their opponents across the demarcation line. Team supporters yelled themselves hoarse as they cheered on their favourites.

Such events still take place, though more sophisticated attractions are gradually eroding the simple, unadulterated sports days we knew in the 1930's.

The main source of year-round entertainment was the cinema. Glittering with lights half-way along Market Street, it was the mecca for young and old alike, attracting like a magnet those patrons who yearned to immerse themselves in the larger-than-life, glamorous world of heroes and heroines who lived out their story-book lives on the silver screen.

We always called it *The Pictures*. The modern, mammoth runs of "Held over for yet another week due to public demand," were unknown to us. Our public demanded, and received, a long program: the main film and a second-rate one; a newsreel and a cartoon, as well as other short features, resulting in a full three hours or more of entertainment, changed in its entirety every Monday and Thursday. The most recent films were shown during the second half of the week, to attract the local business community on their Thursday half-day holiday and also the Friday and Saturday invasion of country people. Young, tanned farm workers came into town dressed in their best suits and purchased their quarter pound of toffees or chocolates before proceeding to enjoy the bright lights of *The Pictures*, either in groups or paired off with girls in the back seats, joining other local couples who had the same idea.

Some patrons, mostly the young and single, saw every program, paying their admission charge twice each week, becoming knowledgeable, at least in their own estimation, about the actors and plots and often offering, welcomed or not, their opinions and know-how to viewers in neighbouring seats.

Admission charges ranged from a few pennies for the front benches to one shilling in the back seats. On Saturday afternoons, for the weekly matinee, the admission price was even lower: two pence for the benches and four pence and sixpence for the better seats. The "twopennies" were often unkindly referred to as *The Flea Pit* and were occupied mainly by boys who scuffled and fought, stamped their feet, yelled and cheered. They sometimes made so much noise that patrons in the back rows were denied hearing the dialogue taking place on the screen. "The twopennies" were definitely not for the timid. The owners of the cinema, a middle-aged man and his elderly aunt, patrolled the aisles on either side of the benches, long, thin canes in their hands with which to reach into the centre of a melée to prod the offenders. Often the sight of the cane was enough to deter would-be trouble makers.

I didn't go to *The Pictures* regularly. It was a luxury to be afforded only occasionally. In addition, some films were considered unsuitable for children, though a good many children did in fact see them and today some of those films would appear tame indeed. Along with my sister and friends, I saw several Shirley Temple films. They were very popular with girls, many of us envying the curly-haired, cute little star. Her films produced a bevy of small girls wearing Shirley Temple hair styles and also brought about a boom in the tap-dancing business. Countless girls tapped away to *The Good Ship Lollipop* and sang about animal crackers in their soup without the slightest idea of what they were. We didn't call dry, unsweetened biscuits *crackers* in the American fashion, we weren't able to buy them in animal shapes and we never ate them with soup as North Americans did, and still do.

I remember seeing Gracie Fields in *Sally In Our Alley*. Gracie, a true, home-grown English star, was in her hey-day at that time and I was thrilled at seeing the film, firstly because it was the first time I'd been to an evening performance and secondly, because I accompanied both my mother and my grandmother; it was the first time I'd known either of them to go to *The Pictures*. My mother had been a keen film fan in her youth and used to tell me about Theda Bara, Rudolph Valentino, Douglas Fairbanks, Mary Pickford and other romantic stars, as well as popular comedy actors and the cliff-hanging serials that were shown every week when she was young.

Westerns, as ever, were popular during our childhood. Tom Mix and Ken Maynard were two of the western stars who come to mind, with those up-and-coming youngsters John Wayne and Gary Cooper then being cast in minor roles. When the good guys began to chase the bad guys and Indians across the plains and shoot-outs began, the encouraging roars from the front benches of the cinema could be clearly heard by passers-by on Market Street.

Gangsters, cops and robbers often filled the screen, stalking each other through underworld haunts and gambling dens with hats brims turned down and guns at the ready, issuing terse commands from the corners of their mouths.

Lavish musicals began to appear, with eye-boggling sets and chorus girls in dazzling costumes who danced with robot-like precision. Casts were enormous and the tunes were the kind that everyone sang, hummed and whistled. Ginger Rogers and Fred Astaire were on their way to stardom; male stars were suave and handsome, their female co-stars sexy and sultry with thin, painted eyebrows, curvy mouths and luxurious, wavy hair. Most of them over-acted, the producers and directors of that era not being fully accustomed to projecting their message and story by voice. We were not long out of the silent film era and in fact, the second feature at many small cinemas occasionally contained silent segments, at which certain members of matinee audiences sometimes jeered. It was like watching television with the sound off.

The newsreels of that era were fascinating because they gave us our only opportunity to see world figures such as royalty, politicians, current sports stars and other famous people actually walk and move about like ordinary human beings. Outside of newsreels we saw only their images in newspaper or magazine pictures that often were somewhat fuzzy. To see the King and Queen walking along and talking to people, even though we couldn't hear their voices, made them appear a little less distant, more like ourselves.

The cartoons of the day were less sophisticated and not as technically good as today's but they were funny and we enjoyed characters such as Felix The Cat, a great favourite. *Felix kept on walking* was a popular tune from the cartoons. Mickey Mouse had just been born and we saw some of the earliest Mickey cartoons.

Most of the films were American and we were quite convinced that all Americans lived like the stars we saw on the screen; they either rode horses out on the range all day, carried guns and fought Indians or talked out of the corners of their mouths like Chicago gangsters. And of course they all lived in luxurious houses! That Americans lived in houses like our own, went to school or work every day and ate ordinary food was something we gave no thought to. Watching films was like reading stories; during those brief hours at *The Pictures* we lived in another world and believed all we saw.

All films were black and white. Colour was in the experimental stage and when it did arrive was hailed with wonder and delight. Screens were small and reels of film sometimes broke, keeping audiences waiting, whistling and impatient, until they were repaired; when the show resumed, it was greeted with cheers. Everything nowadays is so technically perfect and we accept without question the wide screens, natural colour, good, almost understated acting and films so long they need an intermission. We accept too, the fact that they are shot on location all around the world. In old films, Hollywood sets appeared over and over again with a few modifications to suit the film in question and the country or locale it was meant to represent.

Our cinema no longer exists as a mecca for film-goers. Stripped of its glamour, its screen and its seating it was for a few years a supermarket and has now been converted into a bowling alley.

Now that top-rate shows can be viewed in our own homes via the medium of television, cinemas and the films they show have lost some of their former patronage and attraction. Film stars are still pursued by fans, but no more so - and perhaps less so - than rock stars and prominent sports personalities, who for the most part, look and dress like everyone else. The private lives of film stars are laundered in explicit detail in sensation-seeking magazines, and tabloids and no longer resemble the mysterious, glamorous idols whom we placed on pedestals, and admired from a distance during those bygone, halcyon days of the silver screen.

* * * * *

THE WORLD CLOSES IN

I clearly recall the day that for me signified the end of our childhood years of peace and security, the day the world began to close in.

It was a morning in October, 1935. Dressed in my school uniform of navy blue gym tunic and white blouse, black stockings, velour brimmed hat and school blazer, I cycled, as I did every school morning to the railway station, a satchel of books slung across my shoulder. After leaving my bicycle in a shed near the station, along with those belonging to other daily commuters, I walked the short distance to the train platform to await the train that carried students every morning to their schools in March, ten or so miles distant. I'd begun attending the girls' high school one month previously. Noting that most of the grammar school boys had congregated that particular morning at one end of the platform and were talking and gesturing excitedly, I asked one of the older girls what had happened.

"Don't you know anything?" she replied somewhat condescendingly, then added, "Mussolini has invaded Abyssinia."

No, I didn't know. We had no radio set at home at that time and although I always read the daily newspaper, I didn't usually see it until after I arrived home from school very late in the afternoon. I remember feeling shocked by the news. War! A terrifying prospect, even though that particular war was a very long way away, in Africa.

We had already heard disconcerting reports of the ambitious, strutting little dictator Mussolini, and his fascist followers. Also of Adolf Hitler and his robot-like troops who goose-stepped around Germany, striking terror into the hearts and minds of thousands of people, especially Jews. And after all, Germans were the bogeymen of the Great War, so who knew what they might do again, given the opportunity? Now Mussolini had actually attacked and invaded Abyssinia without officially declaring war on that country.

At school that day there was a great deal of discussion of the new war and teachers tried to fill us in on some of the geographical and historical background of Abyssinia, a country known today as Ethiopia.

The emperor, Haile Selassie, a swarthy, bearded, slightly-built man often photographed wearing a dark, gold-braided uniform, became a heroic figure prominent in the news; his army defended the capital city of Addis Ababa for several months before it finally fell to the attacking Italian troops. We followed daily reports with interest and sometimes with horror as we read of the massacre of monks and an archbishop and of similar attacks on innocent citizens. Haile Selassie was forced into exile and was unable to return to his country for many years.

Fascism was a topic we'd heard discussed and had read about, but to which until that time we'd paid little attention. Mussolini's troops were referred to as Blackshirts and often perceived as objects of ridicule, strutting and play-acting.

From that time there seemed to be no real peace and security ever again. After Abyssinia came further threats and posturings by Mussolini. Adolf Hitler continued his purge of the Jews in Germany. The Spanish civil war broke out. Then came Czechoslovakia and the uneasy peace of 1938. In England that year young men were conscripted into a militia and preparations were made for civil defence, as though we knew war was inevitable. Poland was invaded in 1939 and finally we were officially at war, only a little over twenty years after the Great War had ended. To our parents' generation those twenty years must have seemed so brief a respite, just long enough to see their sons grow to military age, to watch them go as their fathers before them had gone, to serve their country.

At first we tried to convince ourselves that it wouldn't last, that as everyone had predicted in 1914: *It will all be over by Christmas.* Even as they spoke those hopeful words, most people didn't believe them in their hearts; they knew the war would last a long time.

Young men volunteered for the armed forces, not waiting to be conscripted; air raid shelters were built; gas masks were issued to everyone and initially we were required to carry them at all times, in a cardboard box slung by a cord over our shoulders. We soon dispensed with that, having decided the Germans had no intention of killing us off with poison gas. Small children were issued gas masks with Mickey Mouse faces to allay some of the fear of wearing those suffocating, rubbery protectors and babies had to be placed in cumbersome contraptions that covered the top half of their body. We had one of each of those in my family, for my two youngest sisters, one aged three, the other a baby only a few months old.

As soon as war appeared imminent and it was feared that London and other large cities might be bombed, thousands of school-age children were evacuated to the safety of villages and small towns all over the country. As a result, a large number of children came to our town, together with their teachers; there were also a few families of mothers and children who had decided to remain together. The fathers of those families were in the armed forces or working in war-related jobs or would soon be in the London fire service, fighting the fires that burned night after night once the bombing began.

The evacuee children arrived by bus and train, wearing labels that identified them by name and school, and carrying a bag of clothing and perhaps a favourite toy. Local families suddenly expanded as their spare rooms were filled by the evacuees; everyone did their best to ease the children, often very young, over the trauma of sudden separation from their families and homes. To children who had hitherto known only city streets the country was a strange place indeed with its quiet atmosphere, open spaces and fields, farm animals that many of the children saw for the first time and vegetables dug from a garden instead of purchased from a shop or street vendor's barrow. Irksome at first to many of the evacuees was the country custom of going to bed early. But they soon adapted to their new life, their Cockney accents were modified, they quickly made friends with local children and with their adoptive brothers and sisters. It was a great experiment and experience in human relationships. The London mothers descended on the town on Sundays to visit their children and when at first the expected bombing did not materialise, some took their children back to the city, only to return them when the bombs began to fall.

As soon as war broke out there were strict regulations regarding lights; all our windows were covered with hastily-made blackout curtains. Air raid wardens patrolled the streets after dark, knocking on doors if a chink of light was visible, shouting instructions to black it out. Street lights went out for the duration of the war; flashlights, bicycle and vehicle lamps were hooded to cast the beam of light to the ground. Thus were towns and villages all over the country made invisible from the air. At least, we hoped they were! Food rationing was introduced and later, clothing too, had to be bought with strictly-allocated coupons. We used all our ingenuity to stretch the precious rations and coupons, but most people managed well. Making something from almost nothing had been a way of life in the 1930's and the experience stood us in good stead during the war years.

We used to lie in bed at night and listen to the throbbing engines of the German bombers as they flew overhead on their way from the coast to bomb industrial cities in the heart of England and we speculated which city was destined to be the target for their deadly cargo. Moonlit nights, so wonderful for people finding their way around in the blackout, were dreaded by those who lived in target areas. *Bombers' Moon* was how a bright, moonlit night was often described; buildings, rivers, streets, railways, bridges and other landmarks stood out clearly in the clear, stark light of a full moon.

When our own aircraft began to bomb German targets we sometimes heard them as they set off on their dangerous journeys from airfields that were a war time feature of the flat, East Anglian countryside. In the early morning hours we occasionally heard returning bombers limping home, possibly damaged and perhaps with dead or wounded crew members aboard, pilots coaxing their aircraft on that last, long, tiring leg back to home base.

On one occasion, I recall it being a Sunday morning as everyone was at home, we heard, much later than usual, the then familiar, uneven throbbing of a low-flying, damaged aircraft. One by one, families emerged from their houses into the street, standing with up-turned faces. Very low flew the wounded bomber, slowly, haltingly and we held our breath, no one speaking, every eye on the dark shape above us. Two of its four propellers were still, part of its tail hung precariously and we marvelled that the pilot had brought it back across the sea. Slowly it passed and after it had disappeared from view we still stood, listening, thinking of the young men inside, some perhaps wounded and of the anxious waiting at the airfield they were headed for, where hope must almost have faded for their safety. Gradually we dispersed and someone commented, "They'll be all right now. They'll get back." Somehow those few words comforted us, as though the prayers of those watching from the ground along its homeward path would hold the bomber in the air.

Later in the war, soon after the R.A.F. and other Allied bombers had returned, United States airmen set off on their daylight raids. There were several U.S. bases in the Peterborough area and I recall often seeing squadrons of Flying Fortresses as I was on my way to work. I remember how the huge bombers glinted like hundreds of silver, daylight stars on sunny mornings, filling the sky, a massive display of strength. They returned late in the afternoon and like the R.A.F. in the early morning, many of the planes often came home damaged, the crews exhausted from the strain of a day spent avoiding anti-aircraft guns, enemy fighter aircraft and suffering from sheer fatigue, but grateful to be alive, to have come home safely one more time.

I recall that one night, quite late, we heard the sudden noise of anti-aircraft gunfire. There were several gun emplacements deployed in the vicinity of the town, but action in our usually quiet zone was so unusual it was an event. We rushed outside to see what was happening. The sky, as so often on dark nights, was criss-crossed with long beams from the gun batteries' searchlights; suddenly, just a hundred yards or so away, flying at no more that tree-top height across a field that bordered the back gardens of our street, was a German aircraft, its distinguishing black cross clearly visible. Caught in the beam of a searchlight it sped away across the flat countryside, making for the sea and home. It escaped the flak, being far too low to be hit by gunfire.

Gradually the tide of war turned in favour of The Allies and in May 1945, after almost six years of seemingly endless battles, setbacks, defeats, advances and victories, the war in Europe was over. A few months later the Japanese surrendered and the people of the world began to pick up the pieces of their lives and attempt to put them back together again.

The dead were counted and mourned and families learned to live without the husband, son, father or brother who lay buried in a foreign field or who had no grave. Prisoners-of-war were repatriated and reunited with their families. The maimed and wounded began their painful adjustment to a new, more difficult way of life. Young children learned that the stranger who came to live in their home was their father, the cardboard face in the picture on the sideboard now a reality. The last of the evacuees returned to their bomb-scarred cities, with a few families remaining in their war time home, having decided they preferred a quieter, more leisurely life style. German and Italian prisoners-of-war, some of whom had become a familiar sight as workers on local farms, were repatriated to their respective countries.

Some of the Italians, joined by many of their countrymen, returned within a few years as immigrants, most to work in local brickyards, bringing with them unfamiliar Latin names to mingle with the centuries-old British names we'd always lived with. Adding to the ethnic patchwork and introducing further new and sometimes unpronounceable names came displaced persons from the labour and concentration camps of Europe. Those victims of Nazi terror wandered the length and breadth of Europe after hostilities ceased, searching for a haven where they could put down the roots of a new life and raise families in peace.

Servicemen returned home and after the years of separation, marriages were either strengthened or broken, the partners either picking up their lives where they had left off years earlier or filling the divorce courts of the land, forcing a drastic review of divorce laws. Reunited families and newly-weds alike searched for places to live and found none; they had to settle, most of them, for a bedroom in the home of either the husband's or wife's parents or if they were lucky, a room or two in a stranger's house, sharing kitchen, bathroom and all other facilities with their landlord. Local authorities began to plan and build housing for which waiting lists grew to phenomenal proportions as families waited, sometimes for years, to occupy a private, coveted space of their own. Most marriages survived those difficult years and heart-breaking conditions; some did not.

As war time building restrictions began to ease, houses were built for those who could buy, rather than rent. Many married women had prudently saved their marriage allowance during the war and with the addition of their own savings and perhaps their husbands' gratuity received on leaving the services, they were able to buy a house of their own, with a mortgage stretching far into the future.

Food rationing remained with us for several years after the end of the war, some items, such as meat, becoming even more strictly rationed. There were times when we wondered who had won the war. But gradually, as supplies became available, foods were de-rationed, although it was not until the early 1950's that we were finally able to discard our ration books.

When I was a child I used sometimes to stand at the war memorial and read the list of names of those men who had given their lives in

The Great War. The flowers and poppy wreaths at the base of the monument were a reminder that those names had once belonged to real people, to men who had lived in the town, who had gone to work every day and had been part of the local tapestry. But I could not visualise them that way. The fighting men of that war merged in my mind as a composite soldier in a belted, khaki uniform, puttees wound around his legs below the knees, peaked cap pulled low over his eyes, back ramrod straight, waxed moustache adorning his upper lip and brass buttons gleaming as though he were perpetually on parade.

My father had been just too young to serve in that war but some of his brothers had done so, as did my maternal grandfather, who had been over forty years old when the war ended. They all survived. From my grandfather I heard stories of the trenches, the mud and barbed wire, the poppies that grew in Flanders' fields, and of the big guns that could be heard in England on a still night. I heard about battle-shocked men who cringed at every sound; of no man's land and being close enough to the German trenches to hear the mens' voices; and of going "over the top", each man knowing the following few minutes might be his last on this earth. Still, even with those and many other stories of bravery and comradeship and battles, The Great War never seemed close or real.

After our own war, after the new names had been engraved on the war memorial, it was different, very different.

Those new names were no mere alphabetical list. They were faces and voices and personalities, boys I and my contemporaries had played with and been to school with or lived next door to; they were youths we had giggled and flirted with; men we had dated, loved, courted and married. Some were fathers who had barely known their children. The names evoke varying remembrances: a familiar face in a crowd or on the street; a slight acquaintance; a friend's brother; friendships and kinships and long associations; and a few, special memories that will be retained as long as we live. One in the latter category was my youngest uncle who often seemed more a cousin or older brother. Ronald A. Brown went down with the ship on which he served in 1942, leaving a widow, a four-year-old daughter and a new-born son.

Unlike we who remember them, they remain forever young. To read their names is to return to the days of our childhood, to the far-away days when wars were seen as history. We remember those long-ago friends whipping their tops along a street, playing games of marbles in a corner of a playground, grinning across a classroom, taking part in Boy Scout activities, singing in church choirs, playing football and cricket or talking to us on street corners. They are, and always will be a part of our lives and never, never just an alphabetical list of names.

When our grandchildren stand before the war memorial, do they see a composite, keen-eyed second world war fighting man in battledress and steel helmet, landing on beaches, driving a tank, foot-slogging through forests, deserts and jungles, dropping bombs on enemy targets or firing torpedoes from a fighting ship?

* * * * *

EPILOGUE

The world is no longer far away: even outer space, once fictional and unreachable, is now real and close, beamed into our homes by television cameras.

The market place and main streets of Whittlesey are no longer, as they once were, the hub of a small universe, thronged with crowds of shoppers at weekends. Residents now travel to the nearby city of Peterborough to do much of their shopping. Once, that seven mile journey by bus was an adventure, bumping over non-too-smooth roads and old, humped-back bridges along stretches of open countryside. It now takes only a fraction of the time by car, even the distance having been reduced by new roads and straightened curves. Houses stand on some of the areas we remember as open country and one could be deluded into thinking our town has become a dormitory-suburb of the city.

That is not so: it remains a separate place and retains its distinct fenland character and atmosphere. The historic churches and other old buildings are a constant reminder of our past and of the fact that for centuries the town was an important centre for the farms and villages of the surrounding area. Some of those who shared my childhood years still live there, including two members of my own family. Others, like myself, return periodically to visit relatives and friends and to reminisce about what our grandchildren call *The Olden Days*.

It is sometimes difficult to equate the lamplit houses, horse-drawn vehicles, gas-lit streets and small school buildings of the 1920's and 30's with the town in its present form. Entire streets of houses and cottages have been demolished and new streets built where none existed during our childhood. Many families of the now expanded population reside in modern housing developments and their children attend large, bright, well-equipped schools. But with a little imagination we can see places as they were when we were children.

Writing this narrative has been a nostalgic, often poignant journey back to the days of my childhood and I hope that readers who shared similar experiences have also found it so. I trust too, that younger readers have enjoyed the reminiscences and will perhaps ask their parents and grandparents to tell them stories about their childhood.

Thank you for accompanying me along this road of memories.

* * * * *